# Proud to wear my South Side cap

*My half-century journey through nursing*

## Ruth A. Bershok

This book reflects my nursing career
from 1958 to 2017. All events are depicted as I remember them,
but a few names have been changed.

In memory of my dear friend and colleague
Patricia Thomas, better known as PT.

Her caring and compassionate nature was epitomized in her love
of life and the manner in which she fulfilled her nursing career.

# TABLE OF CONTENTS

# PROLOGUE

"What else do you do, Grandma?" I had just described my first few minutes at work—how I receive the report from the 3pm -11pm super-visor and begin my night shift by making rounds to all the units. My 10-year-old grandson was interviewing me to earn a Cub Scout badge. He had to speak to a professional who saves lives and then write a paper describing their day-to-day work activities. I was at the end of a nursing career that spanned over 50 years.

Responding to his questions, I explained my supervisory duties, such as managing staffing levels, obtaining medical supplies, and speak-ing to patients' families. My grandson paused to take notes. "What else?" I explained my hands-on nursing duties, how I start IVs and emergency EKGs, how I attend all codes, how I administer medicine and blood transfusions. He was a thorough interviewer. "OK, got it; what else?" Pressed by my grandson, I continued in my response.

After this went on awhile, my son laughed. "Well, looks like she's done everything except open-heart massage." With his words, my mind flashed back, and I recalled the feel of the heart in my hand. "Actually," I replied slowly, "I've done that too."

My thoughts took me to a busy emergency room. The patient was in cardiac arrest. I was one of two nurses who, along with a respiratory therapist and doctor, were performing CPR. No response. Just when I thought the doctor would call it, he instead made a bold decision. "I'm going to open the chest." He took his scalpel and began. Once the chest was opened, he started massaging the heart with both hands, one on each side. I stood on the other side of the patient and observed the monitors behind the doctor. The respiratory therapist was at the head of the patient, "bagging" the lungs. After about 40 seconds, the doctor directed me: "Take over for me here!" I felt the adrenalin rush and dutifully reached both hands into the patient's chest, one on each side of the heart. I rhythmically squeezed the heart between my hands. As the respiratory therapist squeezed the ambu bag, the air inflated the lungs. It was a weird feeling as the patient's lungs crept over my hands pressed against his heart. We continued this procedure another few minutes, until the doctor called it. I knew we had done all we could.

When I entered nursing school in 1958, I could not expect that I would be called on to do open heart massage nor many of the other experiences that lay ahead of me in my nursing career. This book traces that journey—from 1958 when I was a young nursing student, worried about displaying expected etiquette in the presence of doctors, to 2017 when I said my retirement farewell to my wonderful staff at a community hospital. The nursing journey is different for all who have taken it, but those who have traveled it will understand the joys, the dedication, the camaraderie, the heartaches, the administrative challenges, the frustrations, and ultimately the soul's enrichment reflected here. And those who, like me, have been on the journey for a few decades will appreciate the significant changes, not only in medical technology but in professional attitudes. I hope this book allows the reader a glimpse into that world. I wish a blessed journey to all my fellow nurses who may be reading!

# CHAPTER 1

## *Earning our Caps*

It was mid-summer 1958, and the strong afternoon sunlight highlighted the age of the old brick building that would be my home away from home for the next three years. My father had driven me to South Side Hospital School of Nursing in Pittsburgh, Pennsylvania, about 25 miles from my hometown of Canonsburg. The program was year-round for a full 36 months. We parked on the sidewalk adjacent to the nurses' residence; there were no hospital grounds. As my father pulled my suitcases from the car, I observed the other students walking the steps to the entrance. Like me, most were dressed in heels and calf-length skirts. My father carried the suitcases up the stairs and placed them before the receptionist's desk in the entrance area. When an upper-level student came to escort me to my room, my father and I said our goodbyes. My father could go no further, even to help me with my luggage; no men were permitted past the receptionist's desk—Rule #1. As I would soon learn, there were many rules here.

My father was very proud that I was going to be a nurse and was happy to let people know of my selected career. He would tell everyone he met. Once, when I was a senior in high school, my father was in the hospital with a heart condition. I was visiting him when the doctor came in to do an EKG. The doctor recommended that I leave while he performed the procedure. It was my father who spoke first. "She's going to be a nurse. Can she stay and watch the procedure?" The doctor smiled. So, I stayed while he good-naturedly explained step by step the procedure as he performed it. I carefully observed my first lesson in the medical field.

However, I have be to honest. Nursing was not my first career choice. When I was in grade school, one of my neighbors was a teacher. She let me help her prepare her classroom before the school season. I loved to do this. I would sharpen yellow pencils, organize books, decorate the classroom, and do whatever else she needed done. Once, I asked her for a few old books that were being thrown out. She obliged, and I used them to teach my dolls and stuffed animals. I held classroom in my attic playroom. Using boxes, I made chairs for my class. Each doll and animal had its own seat facing me. I had about eight "students." With the books my neighbor gave me, I read to the students. I asked them questions, and imagined their hands raised. "Miss Wagner! I know the answer!" I corrected the students when needed. I'm sure I held a hundred classes in that small attic room.

I was about fourteen when I realized that my dream of being a teacher was not likely to materialize. My parents did not have the financial resources to pay for a college tuition. My mother was a store clerk at a dress shop near our home. Her salary was minimal. The store owner tried to offset the low wage with discounts on clothes. My mother had magnificent hats and gloves beyond her economic status. My father was a painter by trade, but heart and lung conditions eventually prevented him from climbing ladders, so he took a janitorial job while I was in high school. From my view as a teenaged girl in the mid-50s, I had only a few choices for career: teacher, nurse, secretary, store clerk.

With my father frequently in the hospital, I would observe the nurses who attended him. After I realized that teaching was not a viable career option, I became curious about the nursing field. I watched the nurses use their skills to benefit the patients, to help make them comfortable, to improve their conditions. It appealed to me. One of the members of my church was a student nurse at South Side Hospital. I asked her all about the nursing program there. She gave a positive response. She told me South Side was a great hospital to train at; students get a lot of practical experience. I was encouraged. At that time, the three-year nursing school programs were a lot less expensive than a university degree. Later, I realized why this was. We student nurses spent at least half of our program time working in the hospital associated with the school; we provided valuable labor. Yet, even with the lower costs, I knew my parents still did not have the money to send me to nursing school. The summer before my senior year of high school, I discussed the issue with them. At first, they said, "We'll have to see."

I knew my father would advocate for me. My father and I were close. I was the youngest of three children, and the only girl. There was a ten-year gap between my oldest brother and me, and a six-year gap between my second brother and me. During my teenage years, I was the only child in the house. I was daddy's little girl, and my father wanted me to be able to follow my dreams. It was about a week before my parents gave me their answer. During the wait, I had thought of other options to pay for nursing school, such as working as a store clerk until I had saved enough money. I was relieved and happy when my parents told me that they could send me to nursing school. They had made the very difficult decision to cash in their life insurance policies to pay for my tuition and books. Given my father's medical condition, I knew this was a genuine risk and a sacrifice. This inspired me to do my best. Shortly thereafter, I started the application process.

And, thus, here I was in the late summer of 1958, unpacking my belongings in the student nurses' residence. We each had our own small room, consisting of a single bed, a dresser/desk combination, a chair, a bedside table with a lamp, and a closet. The bathroom and showers were down the hall. There were no personal laundry facilities. The school washed the students' uniforms. Anything else we wanted to wash was usually done on our frequent trips home, or in the bathroom sink. Most of the girls, including me, washed their hosiery in the sink. The classrooms and the hospital's dining room were in the same building. The school nurse also had an office in the residence building. Due to the nature of our work, the school wanted to be sure we were healthy. Each month, we had to weigh-in and speak to the school nurse. The residence building was connected to the hospital via an inside staircase. We could go from our dorms to the hospital without going outside.

After I unpacked, I met with my classmates. There were 26 of us starting the program that year. An upperclassman gave us a tour of the building. I learned a few more rules, many of which I was not expecting. For example, students must remain single throughout the nursing program. Marriage would result in disenrollment. Pregnancy also earned an automatic disenrollment. Further, if we left the building to go anywhere, we had to go in pairs. After I experienced the neighborhood, I agreed with that rule. Also, we were not allowed to leave the residence wearing pants; it was not considered ladylike. I did not agree with this rule. Still, we only broke it on rare occasion, and only when it was bitterly cold outside. Our "house mother," a regimented but caring woman in her early 60s, said, "Now girls. If you put on a pair of pants under your skirt and roll them up, I won't see them. When you are out of sight of the hospital you can roll them down. Just make sure you roll them back up before you come back in." We were grateful that she allowed us this minor rule infraction. Another rule was lights out in our rooms by 11 p.m. The house mother made rounds between 11 p.m. and midnight. She would open our doors, which were always unlocked, and verify each student was in bed and the lights were out. The house mother's name was Mrs. Patterson. Unbeknownst to her, we called her Mrs. Pittypat, because we could hear her walking up and down the hallway each night.

We wore our uniforms both to class and while working in the hospital. The color of the dress distinguished the year of the students. Thus, a doctor or nurse in the adjacent hospital where we did our clinicals would know a student's level simply by the color of her dress. First-year students wore blue and white stripes; second-year students wore solid blue; and third-year students wore pink. All students, with the exception of students in the first six months, wore a cap. All students also wore a white bib and apron over the dress. The instructors told us how to keep our apron from getting wrinkled as we sat in class. We had to fold the two sides of the apron in our laps. We also wore white hose and white nursing shoes. Our shoes had to be polished and shoelaces clean at all times. When the Director of Nursing passed students in the hallway, she would quickly look us over up and down, inspecting our appearance. Students found her intimidating. When I saw her coming down the hallway, I would cringe inside. I had never seen her smile. If she felt some aspect of a student's uniform was not up to par, she would stop the student and crisply direct her to remedy the flaw. We soon began warning our fellow students when she was in the vicinity. Her severity won her a place in a camaraderie song that upper-class students taught us. To the tune of The Caisson Song, the students sang, "We are brave; we are bold; and the whiskey we can hold is a story that's never been told. . . . And if Logan should appear, we'll say, '*Helen have a beer!*' In the cellars of old SSH." There were many songs we learned and sang at South Side.

For the first three months of the program, we had full days of classes, no clinics yet. After dinner, we had study time . . . until 11 o'clock of course. On more than one occasion, I was caught by the house mother for studying past 11. If you had not finished your studying by lights out, you would have to set your alarm clock earlier to finish your studying before breakfast.

All classes in the three-year program were nursing related. We studied systems of the body, disease processes, fundamentals of nursing, death and the grieving process, and many other subjects within the medical field. There were no options in our course curriculum; the curriculum was set. One of the most interesting classes in my three years was also one of the most difficult—pharmacology. We had to learn numerous medications, the disease processes they were used for, proper dosage, side effects, contraindications. This class was an obvious prerequisite before we could administer medications. Before we could administer injections on a patient, we practiced in the classroom. We first started by injecting oranges. Eventually we were ready to practice on a human—a fellow student. We used small needles and sterile water. The instructor not only provided in-class training, but also served as our clinical instructor. At the hospital, she would question us before we went into a room to give a patient a medication. She would ensure we knew what we were giving and why. Under her watchful eye, we carefully drew the correct amount of liquid from the vial, administered the injection, and recorded the medicine, amount, time administered and bodily location. Before we could administer medications on our own as student nurses, the instructor had to observe us flawlessly perform this procedure three times.

My least favorite class was Anatomy. Well, I didn't mind the academic work. But I did *not* enjoy the lab. We started small—dissecting sheep eyeballs. Eventually, however, came the cats. We were told that much of a cat's anatomy—nerves, muscles, ribs—is close in structure to humans. This information didn't alleviate my distaste. And the lab was right before my lunch. The odor of formaldehyde still clung to me when I was selecting my food.

For the most part, the students were serious about studying. If we did not make at least an 80% on a final, we could retake it only once. If unsuccessful on the second retake, *goodbye*. A student who did not maintain at least 80 percent in each and every class throughout the three-year program would be disenrolled.

After the first three months of class work, we started to spend half of the day on the nursing units. We learned basic procedures including taking blood pressures, providing bed baths, changing linens, and giving back rubs. At first, we accompanied a senior student on her rounds. Then we performed basic patient care on our own. We had six to eight patients each. In the morning, we would serve the patients breakfast, change the linens, and set up the water for the patient baths. The complexity of the bathing procedures depended largely on what floor you were on, as it varied with the patients' conditions. But we always provided patients a morning back rub with lotion. This was thought to be good for circulation, preventing bed sores, and relaxing the patient. In the afternoon, we helped patients with lunch, straightened bed linens, and provided additional back rubs. At this time, we had not even earned our nursing caps and could only do these basic tasks. Nonetheless, this time interacting with the patients and the hospital staff was very valuable. We learned the routines of the hospital and how to effectively and compassionately communicate with patients.

My nursing class was fortunate to have a wonderful clinical instructor for these three months. She had a very efficient manner. She would do rounds and check on each student. She observed how we had made the patient's bed—with sharp-looking mitered corners—and whether the patient looked comfortable. But I never feared the inspection. If something was not to exact standards, she never raised her voice or criticized. She would simply explain how to do the procedure better. She would also perform the procedure as she explained it to us. She had a quiet professional manner that put us at ease and made us want to perform our best for her.

The staff knew from our attire—blue and white striped dress and no cap—that this was our first semester of clinicals. Being new, we were taught proper etiquette towards physicians. More rules. Rule 1: If we were sitting at the nursing station and a doctor entered, we had to stand until he gave us permission to sit. Rule 2: A nurse did not walk into a room or an elevator before a doctor. If you approached together, you would stand back and let him enter. Rule 3: If you passed a doctor in a hallway, you had to greet him, even if he were engaged in conversation with someone else and he did not acknowledge you. If you failed, he could report you to the head nurse. I was eighteen years old when I learned these rules, and I had never been exposed to this kind of hierarchal system of prescribed courtesies. I certainly acknowledged the professional expertise of the doctors. However, this mannerism of respect should be earned, not demanded. Yet I obeyed to the letter. This required behavior was not something I would jeopardize my career over. I would not let my father down.

Even though I had this aversion to this required etiquette, it became ingrained in me over the three-year program, heavy on clinicals. Years later, when a doctor told me to call him by his first name, I hesitated. The South Side voice in my head told me I was breaking protocol, not showing proper respect. Eventually, I learned to use physicians' first names when invited, but I was never fully comfortable with it.

There was another habit I picked up during the first semester on the floor, and I never fully broke from it during my career—eating quickly. When we worked the floor, we were given 30 minutes for meal break. Within that thirty minutes, we had to get to the cafeteria in the adjacent building, stand in line, be served, eat, and return to our units. This usually meant we would have about ten minutes to eat a full meal. It was worse at lunch than dinner, given the number of hospital personnel in line. If we returned to our unit late, we risked being reported to our instructor.

Eating quickly, however, was far from the worst habit I picked up at nursing school. One day, as I was waiting in line at the cafeteria, a representative from a cigarette company was handing out free samples to the hospital employees. I accepted a mini pack of menthol cigarettes. The pack sat in my room for a couple weeks, until I had to write a long paper. As a distraction to the long hours of mental concentration, I thought I'd try one. After smoking on and off, I quit for good about ten years later.

While we had a busy schedule as nursing students, we did find time for leisure. We would go for walks—never in pants and always in pairs, as required—and sometimes stop for a milkshake. There was a bowling alley close by that had duck pins, the smaller bowling pins. As we walked there, we could smell hops from the local brewery. There were many bars in this area, a bar or two on every corner. We students stayed away from the main street on Friday evenings, the pay day for many workers; the bars were crowded and rowdy. When the weather was nice, we walked across the bridge over the Monongahela River and into downtown Pittsburgh, or sometimes we took the trolley. We had very little money, but window shopping was free and I particularly liked Macy's. At Christmas time, we made the trip downtown just to see Macy's elaborate window displays.

About once a month, the student nurses had a basketball game with another nursing school in the area. We traveled by a minibus provided by the school, and were escorted by one of the course instructors. These games were purely social. In fact, we never even practiced as South Side did not have a gym.

I would often go home on the weekend. Usually my father picked me up, but sometimes I took the bus. I would spend most of Friday evening and Saturday studying, but occasionally met a girlfriend for a movie or a walk through town. In the autumn, we might catch a high school football game. Sunday morning, I always went to church with my parents. My father sang in the choir, and I sat with my mother in the pews. According to the fashion rules my mother taught me, I always made sure my shoes matched my purse. So, if I wore navy blue shoes, I would carry a navy blue purse. We always wore hats and gloves, even in the summer heat. These also had to match each other. I had many gloves—white, pink, yellow, shades of blue. We wore short gloves for church, long gloves were for more formal occasions. Sunday afternoon, we usually visited with relatives, and I went back to South Side in the early evening.

After six months of training, we had earned our student nursing caps. This momentous passage in the life of a student nurse was celebrated with an official capping ceremony. Six students had already left the program; there were now 20 of us. Students sat on stage, facing an audience filled with family members and friends. I could see my parents, pride on their faces. There was an invocation and speeches were given. Then each student was called forward and the nursing cap placed on her head. When we had all been capped, we recited a version of the Nightingale Pledge. In unison, we said:

> I solemnly pledge myself before God and in the presence of this assembly:
>
> To pass my life in purity and to practice my profession faithfully.
>
> I will abstain from whatever is deleterious and mischievous, and will not take or knowingly administer any harmful drug.
>
> I will do all in my power to maintain and elevate the standards of my profession, and will hold in confidence all personal matters committed to my keeping, and all family affairs coming to my knowledge in the practice of my profession.
>
> With loyalty will I endeavor to aid the physician in his work, and devote myself to the welfare of those committed to my care.

After the recitation of the pledge, we all received a white ceramic candleholder in the shape of a lamp, a symbol of the work of Florence Nightingale and the nursing profession. Music played for the recessional, as we solemnly exited the auditorium, while the audience remained seated. I felt important in my cap; my uniform was now complete.

During the remaining six months of the first year, we wore our student nursing uniforms, complete with caps, both while working within the hospital and attending classes.

# CHAPTER 2

## *Serves*

I peeled my cap from my parents' refrigerator door where I had plastered it to dry. This was a trick I had learned from a fellow student. The student nursing caps consisted of one flat piece of cotton material, with a straight bottom, a center rectangle with a rounded top and two smaller wings. After washing mine, I would dip the wet fabric in a pan filled with liquid starch. Then I took the wet material and stuck it on the refrigerator door. Perhaps the starch helped it stay in place until it was dry. I don't know, but this method worked perfectly. No ironing needed.

After removing the cap from the door, I folded it and pinned it as we were taught to do. Next came the process to ensure the cap stayed on your head while you worked. First, students put a small safety pin in the material underneath the top of the cap. We then secured a bobby pin in the safety pin. Two more bobby pins were required. These were to hold a small square of padding on the top of the head. Many students used a folded facial tissue; I chose the little pad that came with a bottle of shoe polish. Once the bit of padding was in place on the top of the head, we fastened the bobby pin in the hat onto the padding. At the time, I thought this was a fairly easy process. And, comparatively, it was. The preparation of the student cap was much simpler than the preparation of the South Side graduate caps.

I was starting my second year, now wearing the solid blue uniform of a second-year student and, of course, a very crisp cap. I was looking forward to the clinicals, which we called "serves." Through the serves I would acquire knowledge and skills within various medical specialties. Each serve lasted three months. For five days a week, we spent one or two hours a day in class, approximately six hours on the floor, and then time completing homework. My first serve was my favorite of the four—obstetrics (OB). However, this serve did not start off well for me. On the very first day, I innocently committed a faux pas, that left me feeling terrible and served as a lifelong lesson to me.

Day one of the OB serve, I walked onto the unit and was told that my instructor would be late. The head nurse gave us all an assignment. I was to help a woman with bathing. I went into the room and introduced myself and began to fill her wash basin and give her clean towels and a washcloth. To make conversation, I asked her if she had a boy or a girl. She did not look at me, but sadly replied that her baby had died. My heart sank; I wish I could have taken back my simple question. I said I was sorry, told her the tasks I was performing, and finished them in uncomfortable silence. Feeling terrible, I told my instructor about what had happened, and that I had not been told before I went in the room that the baby had died. My instructor was not only extremely knowledgeable about obstetrics, but she was also compassionate and caring. She said she was sorry that it had happened and that she would talk to the head nurse about it. I learned a lesson that morning. From that day on, while giving medical care, I took my general conversation clues from items on the bedside nightstands or from the patients themselves. I tried to get patients to talk about their interests. I often would start the conversation with general thoughts regarding the items I saw, such as "Oh, I see you like puzzles," or "Is this your family?" or "Do you like that author?"

In the three-month OB serve, students worked one month in the patient rooms, one month in the nursery, and one month in labor and delivery. The second month I was assigned to the nursery. This was the best part of the OB serve. I loved helping the nurses with the babies. We would monitor the babies' conditions—their heartbeat, breathing, color. We would wash them, change diapers, weigh them, and feed them when needed. We would take the babies to their mothers for nursing. At that time period, newborns did not stay in the room with their mothers, and a delivery was usually followed by five days in the hospital. In the nursery I especially liked to rock and sing lullabies to the babies when time allowed. Music had been a part of my childhood. My mother played piano, and my father and I sang while we did dishes together. All four years in high school, I sang in the chorus. My senior year, I sang in both the district and the county choruses. To this day, I can recall the warm relaxing feeling of rocking the newborns in my arms and singing "Irish Lullaby," a song I had learned from my parents. The nursery was usually a happy place to be.

The third month of this serve I was assigned to labor and delivery. This was the hardest part of the OB serve. A vast range of human emotions are possible, depending on the course of the labor and the outcome of the birth. In the labor room, I monitored contractions and notified the registered nurse (RN) when I felt the patient needed to be checked further. I had up to six women in various stages of labor at any given time. I tried to be supportive but I really had no idea of the extent of labor pain. I also provided general bedside care to the patients, and under the supervision of an RN, I gave pain medications. Additionally, I gave updates of the patient's progress to their family. In 1959, the family members, *even the father*, were not only prohibited from the delivery room, but also the labor room. Fathers often went home while the mother progressed through labor.

When the doctor directed, the patient was wheeled into the delivery room. Medical personnel would normally consist of one doctor, two nurses, sometimes an anesthesiologist, and the student nurse. I would usually place myself at the head of the bed, and encourage the patient. Looking back, I wonder what these women thought of this 19-year-old student coaching them through a process she had no experience in. After the birth, I would suction, weigh, and measure the baby. Occasionally, I would actually help with a delivery. Once, a doctor was repositioning a breach delivery. I was gowned and gloved, and he taught me the procedure hands on. I felt the baby before it was born. As a student nurse experiencing this area of health care for the first time, the ambiance of these events came full force to me. There seemed to be a bright energy that filled the room with the entrance of a healthy newborn, creating a celebration that radiated from the delivery room. On one occasion, however, the baby was malformed and stillborn, and the subdued somberness seemed to create a vacuum in the room. I still had to weigh and measure the stillborn baby. Then one of the nurses instructed me to take the baby to the morgue. In my serves so far, this was the hardest thing I had to do. I wrapped the baby in a blanket and carried it in my arms. I could feel the warmth still emanating from the tiny body. As instructed, I used the service elevator to go down to the basement. I put the baby on a cold slab in the morgue and delivered the paperwork to the attendant. I have served a long career in nursing and seen many deceased patients, yet this early memory stays clear with me. As a 19-year-old student nurse it was particularly poignant carrying the tiny body, still warm, to the basement morgue. Thereafter, I could never see as routine the birth of a healthy child.

Even though there were sorrowful times in OB, the happy times were much more abundant. This was my favorite place to work in the hospital. It also helped to have an instructor who was not only skilled in obstetrics but was kind and positive. Her energy and compassion were absorbed and retransmitted by the students. She was diligent in her instruction and observation. She provided constructive criticism, but never degraded us, and never raised her voice. She was our model for what a professional nurse should be. I felt more confident on the floor after completing my first serve. And in this, my first serve of my second year, I only broke the etiquette rules once. It was in entering an elevator. I had walked down a hallway, pressed the button, and when the elevator doors opened, I stepped in. The elevator operator gave me a harsh scowl. I didn't understand why, until I heard her say extra loud, "Hello, *doctor*." It was then I that noticed the man behind me and realized I had broken the rule of entering an elevator before a doctor.

During these serves, I got to know a few of the student nurses in the class above me. They were doing their third-year floor work, and occasionally we would have a moment to chat. I found out this class was less afraid to break the rules than my class. They had a system to sneak out after curfew. First, they found a way to exit the residence hall without being seen by the house mother, who was usually manning the desk at the entrance. Because the doors would lock behind them, they arranged a time for a fellow student to let them back in. I could never do this; getting caught breaking curfew could bring discipline from the Director of Nursing. I also found out that one of the third-year students didn't meet the admission criteria—she was married. Her husband was in the military and stationed out of the area. To avoid detection, she did not wear her wedding ring. I wasn't supposed to know; the class was keeping her secret well. One day in the stairwell of the residence, I heard someone mention the husband. Several students from the class above me were sitting on the stairs talking. I was walking up to my floor and had stopped to chat, when it was mentioned that the student was going to see her husband that weekend. Someone realized that an outsider was present. They all looked at me, anxiously. *"You can't tell anyone!"* I promised not to and I never did, not even to my closest classmates. This student's married status was never discovered by the administration, and she graduated from the program.

~ ~ ~

After I walked through the doors on the first day of my second serve, I was shown where the sterile gowns, hats, and booties were stored. I was a bit nervous to begin the operating room (OR) serve. I was aware that some students were unable to complete this serve. Going in, I understood that observing operations was stressful and many surgeons were known to be intimidating. After we donned our attire, our instructor took us on a tour of the operating suite. I could tell right away she would be a sterner instructor than my OB instructor. I concluded that this was due to the nature of the OR, where a small distraction could have grave consequences. After the OR tour, the instructor took us to the training room where different instruments were laid out. We had to learn the names of all the instruments and the applicable type of surgeries. A few days later, she instructed us on how to open a sterile tray without contaminating it. Later we had individual testing. It was at this point that I uncharacteristically spoke out.

I was called into the room for my testing. The instructor showed me different instruments and quizzed me on their names and uses. I did fine here. Then she pointed to a sterile tray on the table. Even while wearing sterile gloves, there is a precise technique we had to follow to ensure the instruments would not be contaminated. It started with opening the tray's wrapping one flap at a time. Apparently, I was not performing this correctly. I heard a sharp, "You contaminated it!" I put the flap back in place and started over. I heard it again. "You contaminated it!" I started again. After the third time I heard her reprimand, the frustration welled up. I said, "Well, if you would *show* me what I was doing wrong then maybe I wouldn't contaminate it." I immediately regretted my tone, and was worried that she would report me to the Director of Nursing for insubordination. Students could be tossed out for such offense. She looked at me with shock on her face but then proceeded to show me how to properly unwrap the tray. The unwrapping was the last part of the test that day. I was thoroughly relieved to walk out of that room.

This prerequisite instruction seemed overwhelming, but I finally got it. Once we completed this phase, we were allowed in the OR. At first, the student nurses only observed surgeries. Thereafter we served as the "circulating" nurse, and, finally, in our last month, as the "scrub" nurse. When observing, we stood on stools to the side of the scrub nurse. Each time I observed, that first incision into the prepped skin made me cringe inside, but then I became very interested in what I was observing. Some of the surgeons were very good about explaining what they were doing. They would explain the condition of the organs as they observed them and the surgical process. I would listen intently. Sometimes these surgeons even invited questions. There were a few surgeons, however, who would not talk to us, either during or after the procedure. We would know beforehand the type of procedure being performed, but not much else. For these operations, I watched the procedure, but I didn't always understand the surgery itself. When I was fortunate to observe a surgeon who did explain the procedure, I always thanked him afterwards.

After a period of observing, we started to "circulate." This meant we were in the operating room and available to retrieve any extra supplies needed during the surgery. There was a designated circulating nurse for major surgeries, but not for minor surgeries. As a circulating nurse, I stood back and observed. If the scrub nurse needed something—instruments, sutures, sponges—she would request the circulating nurse to obtain it. The circulating nurse needed to know where all the supplies were located. Time was of the essence. Often the requested supply would be in the room, but sometimes we would have to go to the unit's OR supply room. We also had to open the package without contaminating the item. My serve group had no issues here; the training of our strict instructor came into play.

In the last month of the OR serve, we performed as scrub nurses during surgeries. Our primary responsibility was to hand instruments to the surgeon. This was done in a certain manner and always using a sterile technique. We started as the sole scrub nurse in minor surgeries, and as our experience grew, we were assigned to work alongside an experienced nurse in more complicated surgeries. There were two surgeons who would not allow students to either scrub or circulate for them. They didn't like students in their operating room. Towards the end of my serve, I was assigned to scrub for many T&As—tonsillectomies and adenoidectomies. Because this was a quicker procedure, we could perform several in one day. At that time, 1960, is was a common procedure performed on children. We would do six a day, two or three days a week. I would scrub my hands before each case, using a disinfecting soap and following the lengthy procedure we were taught. By the end of my serve, my hands were chapped and dry. When I was assigned to T&As, there was not a registered nurse present, and I performed all nursing duties. In addition to handing instruments to the surgeon, I also suctioned the patient's mouth during the procedure. I noticed that I was assigned more T&As than any other type of procedures, and I asked the scheduling nurse why. I was expecting something along the lines that the surgeon thought I had good skills, but I was let down by her reply. "Because we don't like to do them." At least she was honest. However, I felt that my time in the OR would be more of a learning experience if I were assigned more complicated surgeries.

The worst part of the OR serve was not the T&As, but the "terminal cleaning" at the end of the day. When we served as either the circulating nurse or the scrub nurse, we were required to clean and disinfect the operating room we served in. Free labor! With disinfectant, we cleaned everything in the room—cabinets, table, overhead light. We worked from the top of the room to the bottom, so that there was no chance of recontamination. The final step was mopping the floor. This whole process added about an hour to our shift. The students had great teamwork in this tedious daily task. When a student finished her own room, she would offer help to her fellow students. We assisted each other until all rooms were cleaned. At the end of our shift, wearing our blue uniforms but without the student caps (only OR caps in the OR serve), we would take the elevator down to the first floor, walk down the hallway and down the steps to the residence halls, as we chatted about our day.

Although I learned a lot in the operating room, it was my least favorite place to work in the hospital. Since that serve, I have never worked in an operating room. Some nurses thrive in OR, but it just simply did not appeal to me. I think the cleaning bit may have tainted my attitude. There was one aspect of the OR serve that I enjoyed, however—having every weekend and holiday off. I was able to go home for Thanksgiving, Christmas, and New Year's Eve.

~ ~ ~

After the OR serve, my serve team packed our few belongings. Our next serve was not at South Side but at Children's Hospital in the Oakland neighborhood of Pittsburgh, and we would be staying in their residence halls. Several area nursing schools also sent their students to Children's to complete a serve. We all came to Children's because the pediatric unit at each of our hospitals was small. It was felt that we would have a better learning opportunity at this facility. Students in the Bachelors of Science in Nursing (BSN) degree at a local university also performed clinicals at Children's. However, they did not stay in the residence halls, and did not take the same accompanying classes we did; they attended classes at their university.

I was looking forward to a new clinical experience, as well as exploring Oakland. The area near Children's had several ethnic restaurants and stores and was considered a safe area to walk. I was aware that some South Side students took the trolley across town to Oakland, just to enjoy its ambiance. At that point, I had a boyfriend, Art. A fellow student and her boyfriend had set us up on a blind date, to double date with them to a dance. This initial date went well, and Art and I arranged a second date. It was to a Pittsburgh Pirates game at Forbes Field in Oakland. There, I got an insight into Art's passion for sports. While my father and I enjoyed listening to Pirate games on the radio, Art was on a whole different level. He cheered loudly upon countless plays and recorded each play on a scorecard. At one point, he got up to go to the restroom. He casually handed me the scorecard and said, "Keep score while I'm gone." I had no idea how to do this. When he returned, the scorecard was missing a couple of plays. I had to explain to him that I did not know how to record the plays. He replied, "Oh, I'll teach you." I was now the backup scorekeeper and apparently skilled enough for a third date. Oakland provided me not only a rich nursing experience but also a wonderful dating locale.

With my two suitcases and garment bag of uniforms, I reported in at the residence halls of Children's. The nurses' residence was located next to the hospital, but unlike South Side, there was no connecting hallway. The class rooms and dining hall were also in this building. Like South Side, we each had our own room. I was pleasantly surprised with my room, with its clean pastel colors and upgraded furniture. And I had a window, something absent from my room at South Side.

The next morning, the students met in the classroom to receive our books and assignments. After lunch we toured the hospital. I was amazed at how many patients there were and the extent of their illnesses. The patients ranged in age from young infants to teens. We learned the treatment for the various diseases and conditions that were treated at Children's—cystic fibrosis, cancer, cerebral palsy, neonatal, pneumonia, accidental poisonings, and many others. We learned complete nursing care, from medications to bathing and feeding. For example, with the latter, we had a lesson in feeding a child with a cleft palate. I found the hardest subject for me was pediatric pharmacology. There are different formulas for children's doses that we had to memorize. Often, we would have someone double check our math to make sure it was correct.

There was no typical day at Children's. In the early morning, the students had breakfast together in the residence hall and then would walk together to the hospital. Being from different schools, we had different uniforms. Student caps were also different, with some having stripes for each year of nursing training. We would report in to the head nurse of our units to get our assignments. The head nurse would give us the names of the patients, the rooms, and any special information. At the nurses' station, we would then check the cardexes. A cardex was essentially a layered flip file that contained pertinent information of a patient, including medications and treatments to be provided. The cardexes were prepared by secretaries transcribing doctors' orders and checked by the registered nurses.

The student nurses from South Side were typically given a greater number of patients than the other student nurses. One day a fellow student and I were having a busy day. We each had seven patients and were trying our best to administer excellent care to them. We noticed a BSN student had only one patient and was asking for help. We approached the charge nurse and asked why we had seven patients each and the other student had only one. She replied, "Because I know students from your school can do it." We went back to work, not satisfied with the answer.

I worked on two of the floors during this serve. I started on the floor for babies and younger children. I soon found that taking care of children required different focuses than taking care of adults. The children were dependent on someone caring for them. I intuitively picked up lessons in giving TLC. With the younger children that could not yet talk, I had to be extra observant. I tried to be gentle with the children and always talked to them when I cared for them. One afternoon, I passed the room of a little boy, about five years old, who had cancer. I heard him crying. I went in to see what was the matter. He said his mommy was late, and he was afraid she wasn't coming. I tried to reassure him, but it wasn't working. So, to distract him, I sat down next to him and started to read him a story. As he listened to me read, he stopped crying. When we were almost finished with the book, his mother hurried into the room, apologizing for running a tad late. He quickly forgot about me and was all smiles. There is another reason I remember this boy well—his love of hotdogs. Every meal tray, including breakfast, had a hotdog on it. His doctor allowed this, to ensure that he ate something. We were to give him any food he asked for. His prognosis was poor; this saddened me. At that time, hospitals did not have aggressive therapies for cancer.

I was given patients with a broad range of conditions, and, as mentioned, being a student from South Side, I usually had a pretty full load. I brought a lot of energy and focus to the job, as I wanted my patients to receive first-rate nursing care. There was one morning, however, when the head nurse's confidence in me truly tested my student nursing limits. When I reported for work, I was told that my assignment was being changed. The registered nurse working neonatal care called off and I had to work the unit by myself. Having never worked in the neonatal unit, I did not know the complexity of the work involved. The head nurse tried to reassure me. She told me that the night nurse would stay over and walk me through my duties. She also said I could call her if I had any problems. Not being in a position to refuse, I dutifully walked to my unit. When I walked into the nursery and saw isolettes and tiny premature babies with multiple tubes inserted, I think my heart skipped a beat. I questioned my ability to learn the complexities of this care in the short overlap time the night nurse would give me. The night nurse showed me how to take pressure and oxygen readings, give tube feedings and medications, and provide general care to the babies. I was told to call the charge nurse if I had an emergency. The charge nurse did come to check on me twice and gave me a lunch break. There were eight to ten babies, and I did constant rounds, one infant to the next. Afterwards, I was told that I had done a good job. When I left the neonatal unit, I was proud that I had performed my job well, and extremely grateful that no emergency had arisen. However, I still felt that without training in that specialty, I should never have been in that situation. At dinner that evening, when the students chatted about our day, my fellow students expressed relief that they had not been given my assignment.

During the last month of the serve I was assigned to a different floor. My first day on the unit, I heard a strange clicking sound. I asked a nurse what the noise was. She explained to me that it was coming from the room at the end of the hall, where there were two young girls in iron lungs. They had contracted polio and couldn't breathe on their own. While they could make sounds, they could not talk. They were paralyzed from their chest down; they had faint movements in their hands. To get the attention of the staff, they made clicking sounds with their tongue and the roof of their mouth. The student assigned to those patients would respond, and see what the patient needed. When I was assigned these patients, I found that when I attended one patient, the other one would start clicking. In the background was the constant sound of the compressed air. The hospital had set up a mirror on the ceiling angled toward a TV, so these patients could watch the TV while in the iron lung. The hospital had also enabled the patients to read books. The books were set up on stands, and the girls were each given a device by which they could turn pages with the press of their finger. I assisted with their baths and changed diapers. There were arm holes in the iron lung for this purpose. I also helped with the girls' requests communicated through eye movements and nodding in response to questions. For example, they could tell me which TV channel to select. Sometimes, however, it was hard for me to understand what they wanted. In the afternoon we would get the girls up in a chair each with a portable ventilator on her chest for an hour or two. I felt sad for them and wanted to ensure they were as comfortable as possible, but I will admit that I began to feel a bit of strain whenever I heard the clicking start. It meant I would be in that room for a long time.

I felt that I had obtained a large and varied knowledge of pediatrics during this serve. This serve also helped me narrow the field of nursing that I wanted to pursue. As a student nurse in 1960, I now knew I did not want to work in pediatrics. I came to realize no matter how much we did for them, many of these children would not live to be adults. This was a disappointing realization for a 19-year-old who foresaw a career in improving people's physical well-being.

While I was content that the third serve was now completed, I was reluctant to leave Oakland and its vibrant ambiance, particularly knowing that, after brief preparation at South Side, my next serve would be at a psychiatric facility.

~ ~ ~

It was late summer and the beginning of my third year. My father drove me to Woodville State Hospital, about twelve miles from my family's home. As we drove up the long driveway, I took in the several buildings and the large expanse of well-kept lawns. We parked in front of the nurses' residence. As we entered the residence, we were met by an employee who told me the location of my room and the dining hall, and the hour for dinner. I was pleased to find out that all the student rooms were singles as I prefer to study by myself. In my three years of nursing school, I never had to share a dorm room. And at Woodville, I was surprised to learn that the dorm rooms were cleaned daily by the more highly functional residents, as part of their scheduled routine. The Woodville psychiatric facility housed both long-term patients/residents and shorter-term patients receiving rehabilitative treatment.

After unpacking my belongings, I inspected and hung up my student uniform—now pink, as I was a third-year student. I set my cap on the dresser. I always kept it in a plastic bag to keep it clean. At dinner I met up with my South Side classmates, and we met several students from other hospitals. I was surprised how good the food was. We were informed that all the fruits and vegetables were grown on the grounds and tended to by residents. There were always snacks left for us in the evening such as homemade bread, peanut butter, jams and jellies, and fruit. We never went hungry!

Since it was a warm summer evening some of us took a walk around the grounds. We were not yet in uniform. In our casual skirts, blouses, ankle socks, and oxfords, we examined the grounds, chatting about the differences in our school programs and getting to know each other. We were curious about this serve, as we had not yet had our orientation. In our walk, we observed the large garden, the apple and peach orchards, and the residence buildings. We quickly found out there were other creatures living at our residence. Along the front of the building, we spotted several skunks. Later, I was told that the skunks were always there and we should be careful when entering or leaving the building.

The next morning, I put on my student dress, bib, apron, and cap and went down to breakfast with my fellow student nurses. Afterwards, we went to the classroom for orientation to psychology, where we learned about mental conditions and behaviors. There was emphasis on the different types of patients at Woodville and the treatments given there. We were instructed on medications, insulin therapy, and electroshock treatment. We were also informed of behaviors we could expect to see, and our duties in each area of the hospital. We were informed that most of the Woodville patients would remain there for the rest of their lives, but the staff was hopeful that some could go back to their homes after treatments.

As with all other serves, we also attended classes throughout. There were tests and papers to write, alongside our nursing duties. Our instructor would give us our schedule for the month, which listed which units we would be working. My first assignment was on the unit for females who had violent tendencies. This area was a locked floor where the women ate, slept, and spent their day, the latter in a large activity room. In order to gain access, the student nurses, who were not given keys, would ring a buzzer. One of the staff would let us in. My job was to observe the patients and try to communicate with them. I also helped with getting them dressed, ensured patients received and swallowed their medications, and assisted the RN with whatever she needed me to do.

When speaking to the patients, I usually first asked their names. Not knowing what to expect for a reaction, I tried to keep a little distance when I initiated conversations. About half the time, the patient would respond, and I would try to begin a light conversation. There was a younger woman I had a few conversations with. I thought she seemed mentally stable, and I began to wonder why she was there. Maybe she had been misdiagnosed. Then one day, I watched as she went over to a locked window, looked out, and started screaming loudly, "I'm Mary, Mother of God!" over and over again. This was apparently normal for her as everyone just ignored her. She eventually came away from the window and started talking to us again. Her actions made me aware of how quickly a patient's mental state could change, and I became curious as to the trigger for her outbursts. I found the study of psychology fascinating, and enjoyed the classroom instruction.

On one of my first days, I was concerned that one patient needed medical attention. She was standing in the corner staring straight ahead. I went over to her and tried to speak to her. She did not react to me. This was not entirely unusual for the patients here; however, she appeared to be physically paralyzed, not moving a muscle. I went to the RN and told her of what I observed. The RN told me that the patient was in her catatonic state and was fine, and she would eventually come out of it. I kept an eye on this patient. After a few hours, she started to move. I was not used to this broad inability to interact with adult patients, and felt disappointed that my efforts could not improve the patients' conditions. Working on this floor left me with admiration of the patience and knowledge of the staff working in mental facilities.

Since these patients were given medication to keep them calm, I didn't observe a lot of aggressive behavior the month I was there. However, we were instructed not to wear our caps on that unit as they might get pulled off. We also were told never to turn our backs to a patient. I learned the importance of this lesson the hard way. One day I turned around to talk with a patient, while there were other patients behind me.

A woman came up from behind me, pulled my hair, and hit me on the top of my head with her hand. Lesson learned! After that, I paid more attention to the location of patients around me.

My second month, I put my cap back on each day. I was assigned to a different building where insulin and shock therapy were given. I had never heard of insulin therapy and had no idea how this could help someone with a mental illness. As part of the procedure, the night nurse gave each patient a large dose of insulin at six a.m., while the patient was still in bed. At seven a.m. when the students started our day shift, we gave each patient a glass of orange juice and took them to the dining room for breakfast. If anyone did not respond we notified the RN and she would administer glucose. I was informed that the desired effect of this therapy was to keep the patients calm. From my limited time involved in that therapy, I did observe that the patients were calm. However, for many years after, I wondered about the overall efficacy of this therapy in treating the underlying mental conditions involved. Yet, while working the serve, I was not made aware of the underlying conditions or how patients were chosen for this therapy.

These patients ate breakfast in their pajamas. After they returned from breakfast, we got them dressed and took them to the day room. They would watch TV, read, play cards, and knit (with knitting needles issued out for the day). The student nurses would talk with them. To me, most of the patients on this unit seemed mentally stable. Perhaps, the insulin therapy quieted their brain activity; I do not know. They all were very calm. It was quite a change from my first month at Woodville.

While my student group was on this floor, we were called to attend electroshock therapy sessions, approximately twice a week. I disliked having to attend these sessions. The patients did not want the therapy, and it seemed cruel to me. The first day that I saw "Shock Therapy" on my written schedule, I was apprehensive. I knew from talking with the other students that no one liked helping with this therapy, but no one gave me the details before I first attended a session. I entered the room and saw an examination table, the shock equipment, and a station where I would document certain details of the procedure. The only other medical staff was the doctor. The patient was brought into the treatment room. Per instructions from the doctor, I helped the patient onto the table and laid him down. The doctor gave the patient a sedative to help him relax. I remember the patient saying, "I don't want this." The doctor told the patient that he had to have the treatment. I helped the doctor apply the restraints— wrist and ankle restraints tied to the bed. He then applied electrodes to the patient's head. The machine was turned on and the doctor initiated the shock. When the shock went through the patient's body, the upper body arched upward. I was horrified, but remained in my position and continued the documentation. At dinner that evening, I was now one of those students complaining about having to attend these therapy sessions. I emphasized my dismay, ending with "and I have to do this *again* in two days." The reply was simply, "Now you know how I feel."

During the shock therapy, the voltage varied with the patient. I was always relieved when it was over. I would stay with the patient until he or she was alert enough to go back to the unit. When the doctor indicated the patient could be discharged, I would get a staff member from the patient's unit to take him or her back. When the patient left, we would prepare for the next patient. I would usually assist with two or three shock therapies in an afternoon. The students were instructed that the idea was to shock the system back to a normal mental state. According to the staff, it wasn't usually successful.

In the last month at Woodville, I worked in the admissions building. I found this the easy part of the serve. My job was to assist in completing the paperwork for a new patient. I would speak to the patient to obtain the information I needed. First, I had to ensure that the paperwork I was given matched the individual sitting in front of me. I would ask the new patients the reason they were there and basic biographical information. At first, I wondered why most of these new patients were at the facility, as most of them seemed to be coherent and clear-minded as I talked with them. Over time I realized their stories were not always true. However, these patients initially seemed credible, because they believed what they were saying. Documenting the reasons they were at the facility, I would write down whatever these incoming patients told me, even when I was sure it was not the truth. The paperwork was to reflect why they thought they were there. After this initial paperwork was completed, I would escort these patients to a day room. Here, another student would observe them before the psychiatrist began testing.

When I was not interviewing new admissions, my duties primarily consisted of interacting with the new patients in the day room and observing their behavior. I would write down my observations and give them to the RN.

The student nurses had one duty that fell a bit outside the healthcare realm—the weekly resident dance. Our schedules indicated which student nurses were required to attend that week. Residents who were not in a locked unit could attend these dances. A staff member played records; soft drinks and cookies were provided. Student nurses were expected to dance with the patients. My dancing partners usually walked me from one side of the floor to the other side. After we attended a dance, the student nurses were given an extra half day off. We could either leave early on Friday, or return late on Monday. More than fifty years later, I talked to the woman who had inspired me to apply to South Side. She had been two years ahead of me at the school. She did not recall the conversation we had at church back in 1957, but did vividly remember the dances at Woodville. She did not enjoy the dances.

The students went home each weekend; there were no shifts on Saturday or Sunday. Each weekend, I went home to Canonsburg, bringing my books with me to study or write required papers. Usually, my father picked me up on Friday and Art drove me back on Sunday. Art was now a senior majoring in Economics at Saint Vincent College in Latrobe,

Pennsylvania. He would go home to his parents' house in a town about 20 miles from Canonsburg. While I spent much of the weekend studying, Art and I found time for dinners, drive-in movies, and, of course, baseball games. My score keeping skills were improving. I found that I paid closer attention to the games. One of my fondest memories of Woodville was watching Game 7 of the 1960 World Series with my fellow student nurses. After working, the student nurses hurried to the residence hall to catch the end of the game between the Pirates and Yankees. Still in our nursing uniforms, we crowded around the hall's one television, a small screen in a much larger wood cabinet. With the screen about 20 inches off the floor, most us sat on the floor in a semi-circle in front of the television; others stood behind us. We loudly expressed our joy or disappointment over each play. It was a tense game. At the bottom of the ninth, the game was tied 9-9, with Pittsburgh up to bat. We cheered encouragement towards the television when the Pirate's second basement, Bill Mazeroski, approached the plate. Soon, we watched his bat connect solidly with the ball and held our breath as the ball sailed towards the outfield fence. *Homerun!* Yelling with joy, we jumped up and down, laughing with each other. What a great moment!

One thing I liked about the Woodville serve was that we were treated as professionals, as student nurses, not free labor on the side. I discovered I enjoyed studying psychology, and I still find the field fascinating. But I will admit that after taking care of psychiatric patients for a short period of time, I felt myself becoming impatient with them. I knew that this type of care was not my cup of tea. I was sure that I would never pursue a career in psychiatric patient care. Little did I know that I would later work 18 months in a psychiatric facility.

# CHAPTER 3

# *Graduation*

At the end of the Woodville serve, with nine months left in the 36-month program, our class, which started with 26 students, was down to 15. And we soon lost another. One of the students was pregnant and had hidden the fact for a few months. Discovery was inevitable; it happened at the first weigh-in upon our return. She was gone before many of us could say goodbye. We were sorry to see her go, especially after she had put in so much work and effort. We lost one more student before graduation due to health reasons. Our graduating class was half of its starting size. I was careful not to break any rules in these last nine months. Art and I were now engaged, but I hid my engagement ring. Nurses were not permitted to wear rings in the hospital, and I kept mine on a chain necklace under my uniform. To be on the safe side, I wore it under my clothes even when off-duty in the residence. I did not want any questions about my intention to marry. But I did show the ring to my classmates. I knew the fact of my engagement would go no further than their ears. It may seem silly today that I hid my engagement, but at that time under the school's rules and atmosphere, it was the wise thing to do.

The remaining thirteen of us finished the program with its additional classes, more floor work, and preparation for boards. Our floor work now consisted mostly of evening or night shifts. The student nurse was in charge of an entire floor. While there was a hospital supervisor who made rounds, there was now no registered nurse working with me to share her knowledge and discuss patient issues. During the evening shift (3 p.m. to 11 p.m.), I did have two nursing assistants who helped change and turn patients. However, these assistants were not medically trained. During the night shift (11 p.m. to 7 a.m.), I had only one assistant. When the floor was full, a student nurse would have up to 25 patients under her care. This was a lot of responsibility.

Given that we were student nurses and not RNs, there was one limitation. We could not give narcotics without our supervisor's permission. I soon learned that this one limitation was a minor formality. I had two cancer patients receiving round-the-clock narcotics. When I called the supervisor for the first time on each shift, she would tell me that I could provide the patients' medication throughout the shift without further permission. Because intravenous therapy was not used at that time, we gave all medications intramuscularly, i.e. via syringe and needle. The syringes and needles were not disposable. After each use, they were sterilized and returned to the unit. Before we would use them again, we ran the tip of the needle through a cotton ball to ensure there were no burrs. If the tip caught the cotton, we would not use the needle.

Being in charge of an entire floor, I always hoped no issue would arise that I could not handle. As can be expected, however, there were shifts that tested my physical limitations. On one shift, I had a patient who was having frequent grand mal seizures. In attending to him, I could not provide care for my other patients. I called the supervisor, and she came to this patient's room. As I was assisting her, I asked the aides to do the rounds, checking on the other patients. The aides did so, but returned to tell me another patient was seizing. I went to the second patient and observed a petit mal seizure. I called the resident doctor. After he saw both patients and ordered treatment, I followed his orders. After this, I still had to provide medications and treatments to the other patients on the floor. This all had to be done by 11 p.m., so I could give the report to the oncoming shift. We were not allowed to work overtime.

I also had two patient deaths when I was in charge of a floor. One night, an elderly woman died on my floor. I called the supervisor. She told me to take care of it. So, I was the one to notify the family. This was my first experience in notifying a family of a family member's death. Fortunately, the family had been expecting the elderly women's death, given her condition. So, thankfully, the phone call notification was not a shock. I also had to prepare the body for the morgue. I removed the oxygen tent, removed and secured the patient's jewelry, and helped the assistants get her ready for transport to the hospital's morgue. The second death, more tragic, was of a young man who died during surgery. He had been admitted to my floor, but was sent to the operating room, on a separate floor, for emergency surgery. His parents were waiting on my floor for his return. After the OR nurse called me to inform me of the patient's death, I immediately called the hospital supervisor. I expected that she would come and speak to the parents, or that the surgeon would come down and inform them. Again, the supervisor told me to handle it. I was shocked that I was put in a position as the sole hospital representative to inform the parents of the death of their son. As I put down the phone, I tried to run through my mind how to convey the horrific news. I wanted to be compassionate. I remember the shock and agony on their faces as I relayed the information. After the painful communication, I stayed with the family until the surgeon could speak with them.

I did work a few day shifts. During this time, I pretended to like coffee. In our eight-hour shift, the students were entitled to one break—the 30-minute meal break. The RNs, however, took mini breaks on the floor. The head nurse on the floor told us that we could take a quick break in the kitchen if we wanted to get a cup of coffee. So, off I went. The coffee pot was the focus of the kitchen. I knew I didn't like coffee, but I poured myself half a cup and added a lot of milk and sugar. It still tasted bad. I sipped about half of the cup, and poured the rest out. I took a "coffee break" about once a shift.

During the last six months of our program, we all moved into a new residence, which was under construction when my class was performing serves. Like the old residence, this one was connected to the hospital. Our rooms were larger and brighter. And to our delight, each room had a sink. No more washing our hosiery in the main bathroom.

There was also a change in the focus of our classes. We had classes in nursing leadership, covering material such as effective communication, directing staff, and keeping educated in advancements in medicine. We also had review classes covering the material that would be relevant for our nursing boards. These review classes were intense; we were well prepared for the boards. It was during one of these classes that the Director of Nursing spoke to us about post-graduation employment. She said we should work for her at South Side. I thought that was nice of her to express that overture . . . until she continued. She said that she would not give us a recommendation for any other hospital. In her opinion, we owed South Side for our education. Inwardly, I disagreed with this rationale. In addition to our tuition, we had provided valuable labor to the hospital. I knew I didn't want to work under her leadership; I still found her intimidating.

I did have to work for South Side one day after graduation, however. This was to make up a day I missed months earlier. In January of that year, 1961, my grandmother died. When I informed my instructor, she said I could not go to the viewing but could attend the funeral. It wasn't until later that I found out that I had to make that day up *after* graduation; I was not permitted to take a shift on an off day during a normal work week. The rationale was never provided to me.

~ ~ ~

Finally, the day came—graduation. For the first time, the class dressed in the all-white nurse's uniform. No more bibs and aprons. And unlike the student uniform, the nurse's dress had long sleeves. We admired ourselves in the mirror. Directly before the commencement, we were given our graduate caps, completing the uniform of our profession. The graduate cap was not just for one-day ceremonial wear. This was the cap we would wear throughout our entire career—or at least we thought so at that time. Each school had their own style of cap, and nurses would purchase caps from their alma mater to wear on the job. During my early career, I could tell a South Side nurse from her cap. We were the only ones with that particular style. I could also pick out graduates of other nursing schools by their caps. For example, one had a distinctive point, another had a black band across the top, and others had short bands on the side. In contrast, the South Side cap was solid white. In addition, our folds were more complicated and we used four pearl-topped hat pins. The South Side graduates soon discovered that our graduate cap was some-what complicated to fold, much more so than the simpler student caps. It required more time to prepare. No more flattening it on the refrigerator; it had to be properly ironed.

The graduation ceremony took place in an activity room in the new residence, with folding chairs set up for family members. Not only did my parents attend, but my future parents-in-law were there also, even though Art was now away in military training with the Navy. My mother-in-law, who had not pursued a career, was very supportive of me. A few years later, she went through a year-long school for licensed practical nursing and earned her LPN license.

The graduation ceremony began with the playing of Pomp and Circumstance, as we slowly walked down the aisle to our seats. It was an inspiring ceremony. In addition to our diplomas, we received our nursing school pin. I wore mine on the left side of my uniform for many years, up until the mid-1990s when the white nurses' uniform was replaced by scrubs. At the graduation ceremony, I was also honored with an award—Second Best Bedside Nurse. Our instructors had selected the awardees.

After the ceremony and refreshments, students began moving out of the dorms—everyone but me that is. I had to stay behind to make up the one day I missed for my grandmother's funeral. My parents picked up most of my belongings, and would come for me the following late afternoon, after my shift. On this very joyous day, I was the sole person on my now very quiet floor. I couldn't wait to finish that last shift at South Side.

The next morning, I put on my nurse's whites—the dress I graduated in—and my new cap, and reported to my assigned floor. I was hoping for a smooth day. Yet that day would bring me one more face-to-face encounter with the Director of Nursing.

I was assigned three patients in separate isolation rooms. Before I entered each room, I was required to put on isolation attire—a gown, gloves, head covering, and mask. When I left the room, I removed this attire and washed my hands thoroughly. I began the process again when I went to the next isolation room. To ensure the long sleeves of my nurse's uniform would not extend beyond the sleeves of the gown, I rolled them up.

About ninety minutes before my shift was over, I was told that the Director of Nursing wanted to see me. I removed my isolation room attire and plodded down to her office. When I entered, she first made small talk, asking me how my day was going. Then she said matter-of-factly, "I haven't yet received your application for employment here." I was tentative in my reply; my last shift was not yet over. I had already applied for and accepted a job at Canonsburg Hospital in my hometown. After I told her this, she replied indignantly, "Well, I didn't receive a request for a letter of recommendation." I informed her that I could not speak to that, but, yes, I did have a job in Canonsburg. She softened. "If you would like to work one or two days a week here, I would take you." I politely thanked her.

As I was leaving, she stopped me for a final reprimand. "Miss Wagner, roll your sleeves down before you leave my office!"

Later that afternoon, when my parents came to pick me up, I took one last look at South Side. This school had well prepared me for my future career. Yet I felt gloriously free as we drove away.

# CHAPTER 4

## *Boards*

I started working full time at Canonsburg Hospital the week after graduation. My fiancé Art was in Navy technical training in Pensacola, Florida. We talked weekly by phone. We had not yet discussed wedding dates. Meanwhile, I was fully occupied with work and studying for my boards. I lived with my parents, who were both working. They were happy to have me home and supportive of my work and studying. I had a couple of months to study for my boards.

Until a nurse graduate passed her boards and was a qualified RN, she could work as a Graduate Nurse (GN). As a GN, my responsibilities as a floor nurse were essentially the same as an RN. Additional supervision was neither given nor required. A GN's pay was lower, but would be increased once the nurse passed her boards. I worked the day shift, 7 a.m. to 3 p.m. After work, I would study. The review material South Side provided was comprehensive. This material was organized by board subject—pharmacy, surgical procedures and care, medical care, pediatrics, psychology, obstetrics. I also reviewed my student course books. I felt prepared but anxious when I left for the boards.

The boards were held in Harrisburg, the State's capital, about 175 miles away. While many students drove, my close colleagues decided to fly. I joined them. It was a very short flight, but I remember it well, because it was my first airplane flight. I was proud that I could purchase the ticket with my salary from the hospital. The RN candidates stayed at the same hotel, per instructions we had previously received. The tests would be held there, in a conference room set up with desks and chairs.

Our boards soon had a somber atmosphere. Like most of the students, my colleagues arrived the day before the tests. It was that evening that we were told very tragic news. A group of GNs from another hospital were in a fatal car accident on their way to Harrisburg. I don't know how their colleagues made it through the boards.

There were six test sessions spread over three days. We were allowed to take only pencils into the room, no purses, bags or other belongings. After instructions were provided, we were each given a test booklet. It remained closed on our desks until the official timer was started. We had three hours for each test session. Questions were either multiple choice or short answers. After each day, my South Side colleagues and I would meet for dinner. While it was not productive to discuss our test answers, we couldn't help talking about the day's tests. Yet, the conversations only left us second guessing our answers. We also quizzed each other on subjects for the next day. After the final test session, my colleagues and I decided to go to downtown Harrisburg. None of us had ever seen the State Capitol building. It was nice to get away from the testing locale and relax. The next morning, mentally exhausted, we flew back to Pittsburgh and began the long wait for the results. We were told it would take about six weeks, and the results would be mailed to us.

The estimated wait time was accurate. After days of anxiously flipping through the mail, I finally had it in my hands—the envelope holding the key to my career. It was mid-afternoon; I had just returned from my shift at the hospital. My parents were not yet home from work.

I set the rest of the mail aside, and paused before I opened the envelope. I read the results and was not only relieved but elated. A score of 350 in each section was required to obtain the RN license in Pennsylvania. I had scored over 500 in each section! This meant I had qualified nationally; I could obtain a license in any state. States had different required scores. In our review classes, we had been told that California and New York were the states with the highest standards, requiring minimum scores of 500. As it turned out, I later needed this qualification in my nursing career. I couldn't wait to tell my parents. With the letter in hand, I walked down to the dress shop where my mother worked. After I told her I had passed, she relayed the news to all in the shop. I was especially proud to tell my father when he returned that evening. I waited on the front porch until I saw him walking up the street. With letter in hand, I went to meet him. His smile widened when I told him the news. I was a registered nurse at last! My license number was included with the letter.

The next day, I turned in the results to the human resources department at Canonsburg Hospital. My job duties did not change, but my salary did. A few days later, I was asked if I could switch positions with another nurse, a GN who had not passed her boards. I worked on a med-surg floor (medical and surgical), while she worked in OB. It was felt that on a med-surg floor she would gain a wider range of knowledge needed for the boards. I gladly accepted. I loved OB!

# CHAPTER 5

# *Navy Wife and my on again off again start in nursing*

I knew I would enjoy working in the obstetrics department. Given my training at South Side, I was immediately comfortable in OB. The staff was friendly and helped me get acclimated to the unit. I mostly worked the day shift, which I preferred. Little did I know that the job in OB would be my last day shift position of my entire career!

I usually worked in labor and delivery, with most of my time spent in labor. In the labor room, I would listen to the baby's heartbeat through a fetoscope, a specialized type of stethoscope. At that time, we did not have monitors that showed the baby's heartbeat or the contractions. With my hand on the patient's abdomen, I monitored contractions for time and strength. I was not yet trained to do vaginal exams; the more experienced nurses performed those. OB was normally the upbeat place to be in the hospital. I adored seeing the newborns. I was settling into a comfortable routine when I received a call from Art that changed everything.

Art was attending a naval security school in Pensacola, Florida. His commander informed him that he would be going overseas after graduation and completion of the security clearance process. He expected this would be in three or four months, and he wanted to get married before he was shipped overseas. He would be home for Christmas, and thought that would be a good time to have the ceremony. It was already mid-November. I had only six weeks to plan my wedding! And I wanted a traditional church wedding—white wedding dress, bridesmaids, walk down the aisle on my father's arm, reception with friends and family, the whole affair. My mother was not happy about the time frame. She said, "That's not enough time!" But family and friends pitched in, and it all came together. Fortunately, the dress shop where my mother worked specialized in weddings. I ordered my wedding gown and attendants' dresses from that shop, and the seamstress fitted them for us on an expedited schedule. My father worked at the National Guard armory and we were able to rent the large room for the reception. My cousin had a printing business, and she agreed to make my invitations to meet our schedule. The most complicated part was getting the church's permission. The Catholic church in my town had an opening for December 30th. Perfect. However, I wasn't Catholic. Big problem. Art was Catholic; I was Presbyterian. This meant I had to take Catholicism classes and promise to raise our children Catholic. I also received a lecture on my role as a wife. The instructing priest told me that as a wife, I should not work outside the home. I listened politely but inside I had no intention of adopting such a prohibition. The priest requested my family history, asking for my parents' and grandparents' names. I was secretly amused to tell him my grandfather's given name. I looked him in the eye when I said, "Martin Luther." My parents were also interviewed by the priest. My mother told me afterwards that if I were marrying anyone other than Art, she may not have complied. My parents liked Art.

So, it all came together. On December 30, 1961, in a beautiful gown, I walked down the aisle with my father. My two bridesmaids and maid of honor were also beautifully attired. Because it was winter, each maid had her hands in front of her in a white hand muff. Pinned to the muffs, flower bouquets cascaded down. Being that I was not Catholic, Art and I were not allowed past the railing in front of the altar. Thus, we said our vows in front of the railing. After the ceremony, we drove through the falling snow to the armory. Everyone seemed to enjoy themselves at the reception. My mother and I had prepared much of the food. I remember making huge amounts of potato salad the day before. We got the recipe from my brother who was in the Army. The recipe made 100 servings.

At age 21, I was now a Navy wife. Art had to return to Pensacola within the week, so we drove south for our honeymoon. Art loved Dixieland jazz, and suggested we spend a few days in New Orleans. It sounded good to me. While Art and I had been to jazz clubs in Pittsburgh, the Dixieland jazz was different, as Art had promised. I remember seeing Al Hirt playing at a club on Bourbon Street. Walking through New Orleans, I felt on the verge of a new adventure.

After four days in New Orleans, we drove to Pensacola, just a few hours away. Art found us an apartment. It was in a small four-unit one-story building. The owner, an older woman, lived in a separate house on the same property. She was very kind. She made delicious homemade bread, and would invite me over for toast and tea. Art and I had the first unit and another Navy couple had the fourth one. I quickly became friends with the other Navy wife. With her husband out on ship often and Art home only every other day, she and I spent much time together. This was my first time away from Pennsylvania, and I was fortunate to have friendly people nearby.

There was one thing about Florida that shocked me—the segregation. It affected the seating at baseball games, drinking fountains, even the placement of obituaries in the paper. Now I understood what a black nursing assistant told me before I moved down. I had told her that if she were ever in Florida, she should come visit. She replied, "I would have to come in your back door, because of my color." She said this in a serious manner, not as a half-joke. I told her that she would always be welcome in my home's front door. I did not understand the extent of the segregation that I would see. Art, likewise, was troubled by what we saw.

Having planned to work in Florida, I soon obtained my Florida RN license. I inquired about positions at a nearby hospital. Ultimately, however, I did not apply for a position there. First, I had a transportation issue. Art was only home every other day, and I needed to find a reliable means of commuting. Before I could work out that issue, however, I became pregnant and the severity of my nausea and vomiting would have prevented me from performing expected duties. In fact, I ended up in the ER twice due to severe dehydration. Nonetheless, I was certain I would ultimately fulfill a career in my chosen field. I missed caring for patients and the camaraderie of my fellow nurses.

While I was in Pensacola, I received a letter from South Side School of Nursing informing me the nurse who had won the scholarship for Best Bedside Nurse had not used it. So, the $250 scholarship was being offered to me, the Second Best Bedside Nurse in our class. In 1962, this amount would have represented a significant portion of a university tuition. I was again proud of this honor. But it made me wonder, being second best, what I could have improved on. We were never told the criteria or how the awardee was selected. I was grateful for the scholarship offer, but I didn't live near a university so, unfortunately, I could not take advantage of it.

We were still stationed in Pensacola when the Cuban Missile Crisis occurred. When my friend's husband was on ship, he always left his car so she and I would have transportation if we had to evacuate. It was a troubling time. The Navy had a plan for us to follow, but we would have to get to the designated evacuation or shelter site.

My daughter, Beth, was born in December 1962. She would be the first of our five children. Now I knew what the women on the OB floor were going through. Labor cannot be fully appreciated until experienced. We had expected to be in Florida only for a short time, but nearly a year later, now with an infant, we had no departure date in sight. Art had completed his classes, and was waiting for his security clearance. He continued working on base in the meantime. As most of his classmates now had their clearances, we would joke that there must be an issue with one of his scandalous ancestors. In February, his security clearance came through. By that time, we knew his assignment would be to West Germany. But Art still had additional training stateside—one month in Virginia. I accompanied him to Virginia, but not immediately to West Germany. The Navy would not pay travel expenses for Beth and me. It was explained to me that the coverage of travel for family members depended on the rank of the sailor. Art was too low in rank. So, in March 1963, Art left for West Germany and I went back to Canonsburg to earn money for airfare.

My parents were happy to have me back home. I applied again to Canonsburg Hospital. I was up front with the Director of Nursing. I told her that I would only be working a short time, until I could join my husband. I was thankful the hospital hired me under this condition. Because I had a baby at home, I worked the night shift. My parents were home with Beth when I was at work. I worked on a med-surg floor. There were two nurses on the floor at night. We each took one wing of the floor, and each had one aide assisting her. During night shift, we did rounds to check on the patients. Many patients are awake during the night with medical issues and general needs. I gave medications and treatments (dressings, respiratory treatments, special wound treatment, etc.) following the written orders for each patient. After three months, I had saved enough for airfare. I was on my way to West Germany.

Art was stationed at Todendorf. The Navy base was situated within a larger German Army base. Before I had arrived, Art had found us a place to stay in the nearby village of Hohenfelde. It was quite the change from anything I had experienced and far from what I was expecting. The village had two small stores, a church, and a school. The area was farmland that reminded me of Pennsylvania. We rented the second floor of a house owned by an elderly German couple. There was no kitchen on the second floor we rented, nor were there any appliances. I made a quasi-kitchen out of a small room. We bought a German refrigerator which was the size of a small dorm room refrigerator. My stove was a one-burner hot plate. We had a bathroom with non-potable running water. The farmer across the road was very kind to us and told me that I could pump water from his well. During the war, he had been a prisoner of the Russians. He told us that he wished he had been a prisoner of the Americans; he would have been treated better. We got to know him; he called me "Rudd-on" for Ruth Ann. Each day, I took a bucket to his farm, and pumped water for drinking and cooking. I bought two plastic bins for washing dishes. Against my nursing instincts, I used the hot water from the bathroom to clean the dishes. Art's choice of housing was the subject of many of our conversations.

One barrier I had was I didn't speak the language. All four of my paternal great grandparents had come from Germany, migrating to the South Side of Pittsburgh. But they did not pass the language on to their children. This was a conscious decision. They said they were now in America and the family should speak English. While I was in Germany, I learned some Plattdeutsch—the Northern dialect. I did not have formal lessons, but picked it up during my daily activities. By the time I left I was able to communicate on a basic level.

There were only about 35 sailors and 16 wives in our Navy community. We all became close. There was one building on the base called the White Hat Club. It served as the bar, movie theater, party and picnic place, and church all rolled into one. Even the officers went there. At other Navy bases, enlisted clubs and officer clubs were separate. There was a small store on the base, but it only held a few items. We would travel 200 miles south once a month to buy supplies at the large base in Bremerhaven. We stayed overnight on these trips.

With the Cold War at its height, we were not permitted to go across any border without written permission from the Navy. There were even some cities close to a border that we couldn't go visit. Once, the Navy wives planned a train trip to West Berlin. We sought permission, but it was denied. Art also had permission denied for a trip to a West German town. While U.S.-German relationships had warmed since the war, there were many Germans who still retained resentment and viewed the U.S. military as an occupying enemy force. We were often treated coldly when we were in the larger city of Kiel. In Kiel, there was a building that had been damaged by allied bombing two decades prior. The building had not been repaired. The rumor among the U.S. military members was that the local community wanted a reminder for the citizens of the harm the Allies had caused.

One day, the farmer across the road—the one who called me "Rudd-on" —came over to talk to the elderly couple who owned the house. He was extremely upset, and spoke quickly. I could not follow the conversation, and hoped everything was okay with him and his family. I found out the cause of his agitation when Art came home that evening. Art had a serious look on his face, and asked where his military overnight bag was. I told him where it was, and asked him why he needed it. He told me that President Kennedy had been assassinated. Since nobody knew who was behind the assassination, the Navy base went on high alert. Art said Navy personnel may come for him, and he needed to be ready to immediately leave with them. We had no phone. It was a scary time. Beth was not yet one year old, and I was pregnant with my second child. I wondered about our safety and whether the Navy would evacuate us if hostilities arose. The next morning, my landlady beckoned me outside. "Come, come." We walked out to the sidewalk, where she pointed to the school. The German flag was flying at half-mast. That made me feel more comfortable. The next day, when Art came back from work, he said that not only was the U.S. military on high alert, but the German Army base was also on alert. I was eager for news. I listened to a British broadcast on the radio and read the military paper, *Stars and Stripes*, that Art would bring home.

When it was time to deliver my second child, I was comfortable enough to have my baby in the German woman's clinic in Kiel which was less than an hour's drive away. My other option was to go to the Navy clinic in Bremerhaven. I delivered my second daughter, Rhonda, at the Frauenklinik in Kiel. When I was in labor, the hospital staff found someone who could speak some English. Otherwise I tried to communicate with my limited Plattdeutsch. The day after I delivered, I got a roommate, a German who spoke English. She told me her experiences as a young girl in the war, what it was like when the sirens went off and how she felt running to the shelters. Overall, I had a positive experience at the Frauenklinik. The best part of my stay was afternoon tea. We received hot tea and a pastry every afternoon. There was even an exercise lady that came around once a day. She stood at the foot of the bed and demonstrated the exercises I was to perform.

As with the U.S. hospitals that I had worked in, newborns did not stay in the room with their mothers. When my baby was brought to me for feeding, she was tightly swaddled. The babies remained tightly swaddled as they lay in the bassinets. This was a different technique than I was used to. In the hospitals I had worked, when we placed the baby in the bassinet, we covered it with a blanket, loose on top. The babies could move their limbs. Another difference, German women stayed in the hospital for seven days after delivery. However, they allowed my discharge after five, since that was the norm for Americans. When I got home, I removed the swaddling from my baby. Her heels were raw from kicking at the tight wrapping.

After we had lived a year in the village of Hohenfelde, an apartment became available in the village of Panker. This is where the Prince of Hesse had his summer home. He had built an apartment building for U.S. military families. So, we moved again. Now, we had a real kitchen! We enjoyed being around our Navy friends. One of the other wives was also a nurse, currently not working. As it turns out, I was fortunate to have her for a neighbor, as I needed her medical care.

At my apartment, I suffered an electrical burn and cut to my hand. I had tried to remove a broken light bulb from a lamp that I had not realized was still plugged in. A neighbor drove me to base, where there were sailors designated as "medics." I don't know how much medical training they had, but I was not confident in their abilities after they had treated me. The medics applied ointment to my hand and wrapped it. I was not pleased with either their technique or their approach. They wrapped my hand haphazardly and painfully tight. To be honest, they seemed hungover to me. I examined my hand later that evening and recognized that I needed better care to ensure it wouldn't get infected and to reduce scarring. I went to the other nurse's apartment and showed her my hand. She was appalled at the care I had received. She applied antibiotic ointment from her own supplies, and redressed my hand. She did this daily, until my hand showed solid signs of healing. I thought that she and I could do a better job providing healthcare on base.

In my senior year at South Side I had seriously considered applying to be a military nurse. At that time, both of my brothers were in the Army, and it was input from one of them that crushed my idea. When he heard of my intentions, he spoke to my parents. He explained that nurses were not treated well in the Army. They were subject to what we would label today as sexual harassment. With this input, my parents were adamant against my applying for a military nurse position. Because I valued my parents' opinion, I reluctantly surrendered this plan. I would not start a career that my parents disapproved of.

While in Germany, Art and I took several vacation trips. My favorite trips were to Bavaria, particularly Garmisch-Partenkirchen. The houses were decorated with paintings and had flower boxes with bright cascading flowers. People were kinder there and would try to speak some English to you. I started my spoon collection on one of these vacations. We didn't have much money and that seemed like a nice way to have a small memento from the places we visited. I came back with about six collector's spoons. Before I left Germany, I did splurge on one thing.

I bought a beautiful German-made rose-pattern tea set, complete with saucers, tea cups, desserts plates, a tea pot and a coffee server.

In the summer of 1965, we traveled back to the States via an Army ship as Art didn't like to fly. I was pregnant with my third child. Morning sickness and seasickness is not a good combination! We were on the upper deck to see the Statue of Liberty, or as Beth called her, "the lady in the water." We planned to drive back to Canonsburg, Pennsylvania, where I intended to work again as a nurse. However, we stayed in New York about a week while Art completed his final out-processing with the Navy. Since New York was hosting the World's Fair that summer, we thought it would be fun to go and see it, before returning to Pennsylvania. We took the subway, a first for me. At the World's Fair, we made sure to check out the German exhibits; Art was already missing the German beers. The girls had fun on the rides for small children. To this day, I remember the awe-struck feeling of walking along the flag-lined avenue towards the huge Unisphere surrounded by fountains. I wanted to just stand there and take it all in.

~ ~ ~

When we returned to Canonsburg, my parents were happy to see us. I had not seen my parents in over two years. They had prepared a guest room, so we could stay with them until we could find a house to rent. We did the rounds of visiting both my and Art's relatives. Everyone wanted to see the girls. Meanwhile, I sought a nursing position.

A friend of mine told me there was an immediate opening in a nursing home a few miles from our house. They needed a nurse for the evening shift two days a week. This would be perfect for me, as I could work on Art's days off. I applied and was accepted. I was in charge of a floor with about 30 patients. I provided medications and treatments, and, with assistance of aides, ensured the patients were fed. While I was happy to be back working in the nursing field, the patient load at this facility was too high for just one nurse. My shift was 3:00 p.m. to 11:30 p.m.; however, I never got off work before 12:30 a.m. and most often I was there till 1:00 a.m., catching up on charting. I worked at the nursing facility until shortly before I delivered my third child in December of 1965. After Bob was born, I took six weeks off, and during this time applied again to Canonsburg Hospital.

In February 1966, I started working again at Canonsburg Hospital. I felt like I had returned to my home turf. I knew many on the staff, and the hospital had not changed much in the years I was gone. It was a small community hospital with four floors. The first floor housed the emergency room, the chapel and business offices. The second floor had med-surg patients and the operating room. The third and fourth floors were also med-surg, one floor for male patients and the other for female patients.

I got right back into the routine. It felt natural to leave my cap in a locker at Canonsburg Hospital before I departed for the day. Most full-time nurses did the same. We only took our caps home when we needed to clean them. It was outside protocol, unwritten, to wear the cap to and from work.

I worked only two evening shifts a week; these were Art's days off. Working only two days a week kept my professional skills up, and allowed me more family time. There were two nurses to a floor, one to each wing. Each nurse had an assistant. Most of the nurses on the evening shift were young, close in age. We had a lot of similar interests. Although we had individual assignments, the nurses were willing to help each other if needed. I fondly remember those days.

The equipment and procedures, always evolving, differed in many aspects from the year I eventually retired. For example, in the 1960's, we did not have disposable equipment. We used metal bedpans, urinals, wash basins, and emesis basins (i.e. the vomit pans). After a patient was discharged, these items were sent to the central supply department to be sterilized and ready for the next patient. Today all of these items are plastic and disposed of after the patient is discharged. Even syringes—glass at that time—and needles were sterilized and reused. After we had injected a patient, we placed the needle in a designated container for eventual transport to central supply where it would be sterilized.

Gloves were not regularly worn, certainly not for routine patient care. We would always wash our hands after treating a patient. This would not be done, however, when we did rounds to administer medications. We did not have disposal gloves at the hospital, and only used rubber gloves when needed. We would wear these rubber gloves if, for example, we had to treat a patient in isolation or clean messy bodily fluids. After use, the gloves were placed in a container and sent back down to central supply for sterilizing.

Another difference was how we administered oxygen. Oxygen was not piped through the walls as it is today. We had large oxygen tanks, placed on dollies. We pushed these down the hall to the patient's room. We also brought a metal stand with a plastic tent attached. The tent was placed over the top half of the bed and the sides were tucked under the mattress. A tube was connected between the oxygen tank and the tent. Occasionally we could use just a face mask.

The medications were given differently than today at the hospital. Today, the Pharmacy fills each patient's prescribed medicine and dosage; these are then sent to the patient's floor individually packaged and labeled. Back in the 60's, each floor had a medicine room, with cabinets of large bottles of medicine which the nurses dispensed. There was one key the nurses shared. The system worked like this: When a doctor ordered medicine, he would write the order on the appropriate space on the patient's chart. A secretary would then copy this information onto the cardex. The cardex contained all relevant information about the patient. From the information in the cardex, a separate medicine order was documented on a removable card and placed in the cardex. The medicine, dosage, and time to be given was on the card. At the shift change, referencing the cardex, the outgoing nurses would give report of each patient to the nurses coming on shift. The oncoming nurses would then prepare a worksheet documenting patients' upcoming treatments. Then the nurses would remove the medication cards and cross-reference with the information on the cardex, to ensure the information had been transcribed properly. Before administering medications, the nurse would take the cards to the medicine room. She would "pour" (as we called it) the meds for all her patients who needed medications that hour. She would put the correct medicine in a small disposable cup with the card and put it on the medicine tray. She would then take the tray and give the patients their medications. On one tray, we could place approximately 20 patients' medications. Looking back, there was no accountability for the medication supply. Narcotics, however, were carefully checked each shift by the charge nurse. She had to ensure that the number of vials and pills remaining in each bottle matched the information on the narcotic sheet prepared by the nurses who dispensed the medication. If there was a discrepancy, the shift nurses could not leave until it was resolved.

The cardex was essential to a nurse's work. If a treatment was not on the cardex, it would not be done. After I retired, I met a fellow retired nurse who had worked at the same hospital. We talked about the cardex. She said, "It was our bible. I couldn't work today; they don't use the cardex." There is one wonderful thing I would note, however, about the loss of the cardex. Doctors now input the orders electronically in the computer. This means there is no cause for error in interpreting their handwriting. While the quality of doctors' handwriting is a common joke, this did create real issues for the staff. I recall many times looking at a handwritten order with another nurse, both of us trying to decipher the writing, saying to each other, "Well, what do you think?" If it was not clear to us, we would have to call the doctor. We'd always get a solid answer, but it was clear that most doctors were not pleased we had to call them.

Even though equipment and procedures have changed over the years, the quality of care I gave my patients never changed. I always sought to provide the best care that I could. It gave me satisfaction to see their health improve.

I worked the 3 p.m. to 11 p.m. shift for two years, and was enjoying the routine. Then one day, out of the blue, Art said to me, "I want us to move to California." He thought it would be like Florida, with its nice weather, beaches, and friendly neighbors, but without the segregation. He was determined to make the move West. I was reluctant to leave my friends and relatives, especially with three small children, but I started planning.

# CHAPTER 6

# *California*

I looked out the car window at straight flat streets lined with palm trees and mountains appearing faded behind a screen of smog. California. We're really here! The excitement Art had for this adventure did spill over to me, but I did have some worry, particularly over getting a job. First, I had to get licensed in California, a process I had yet to start.

We were fortunate that a friend lived in the Los Angeles area and graciously let us stay with her until we found an apartment. She was the Navy wife who had lived in the same apartment complex as us in Pensacola. We had much to catch up on. While she and I caught up, Art went apartment seeking. I hoped he would choose better than he had in Hohenfeld, but with three small children I decided not to accompany him on the search. Ultimately, he did alright. He selected a large apartment complex in Panorama City, in the San Fernando Valley. While Art began his job, which he had lined up before the move, I had yet to start looking for a nursing position. I soon found out from a neighbor that there was a hospital just a few blocks down the street. It was a small private hospital, owned and run by doctors. I walked down and talked to the Director of Nursing about a job. She said she had a position open, and that it was the night shift. She gave me information on applying for my California license. I started the application process that day. The hospital sent for my board results and school records. With my 500+ Board scores, I knew that I would not have a problem getting the California license. There was one aspect of the process that I was not expecting, however. I had to be fingerprinted. Within a month, I received my California license in the mail, and I began work as an RN in California.

It was 1967. I worked the night shift on a med-surg floor, with approximately 30 patients. In addition to me, there was a charge nurse (i.e. the floor's supervising nurse) and a nursing assistant. I mainly gave medications and treatments, such as monitoring catheters, changing dressings, and administering breathing treatments. After I had worked there about a year, a significant change in nursing care was introduced. Cardiac monitors were starting to be used in hospitals. The hospital converted two patient rooms into a four-bed room for patients needing cardiac monitoring. Each bed had a monitor above it. However, there were no corresponding monitor screens at the nurses' desk, as there is today. We were told to check the monitors in the room every half hour. So, we did. The problem was we were never trained in how to read them. The other nurse and I obtained a book on cardiac rhythms and tried to teach ourselves. I reverted to checking the patients' condition as I had been taught in nursing school—vital signs, difficulty in breathing, level of responsiveness, changes in skin color. I did continue to check the monitors, and compare the rhythm to the pictures in the book.

While we were not taught how to read the monitors, we were taught how to use the defibrillator paddles to shock the heart into a normal rhythm. This was fairly new technology, one that was not in use when I did my nursing serves at South Side. In fact, cardiopulmonary resuscitation (CPR) was not a standard procedure performed at that time. When a patient went into cardiac arrest, the patient was pronounced dead. There was no thought of "reviving" the patient. I recall the first time I heard of CPR being used. I was a third-year student nurse, and all the staff on my unit were talking about an incident that occurred the day prior. An intern who had learned CPR in medical school performed the procedure on a patient that had gone into cardiac arrest. He revived the patient using this new procedure. The patient's physician was not present when the procedure was performed. When he found out about it, he became angry and reprimanded the intern for using an unapproved procedure on his patient. While the fact that an intern had revived an arrested patient was the subject of lively conversation among the student nurses, we did not have insight into the procedure itself. CPR was never taught at South Side before I graduated in 1961.

I was intrigued by the new technology of the defibrillator. And, as it happened, I was the first to use the paddles at the hospital. One night while checking the patients in the cardiac monitoring room, I noticed a female patient not responding. The monitor had a strange pattern on it. I checked for a pulse; it was weak and irregular. The hospital did not have an ER, and there were no doctors in the hospital during the night shift. So, I initiated the procedure we were taught. I put the required gel on the paddles and charged them. I placed the paddles on the patient's chest and shocked her. Her heart responded. The pattern on the monitor became normal again. I was amazed at the results of this new technology. But the patient was not grateful. She later yelled at me, because she had a small burn on her chest. I tried to explain the procedure to her and the amazing results. She only yelled at me and told me to get out of the room. I had to have the other RN take care of her after that.

Occasionally we had famous actors as patients; some were admitted under aliases. Most of them were quite pleasant patients, but I had one who was very demanding. Nothing pleased him. He did not like the room. He didn't like the hospital bed, and he told me that he wanted his own bed brought in that night. This was a first for me. I didn't know what he expected me to do, so I told him that maybe he could arrange for his bed to be brought in the next day. When he wanted more pain medication than prescribed, he got angry at me and demanded that I call his doctor (which I did). The next time he was admitted after surgery he had a private duty nurse. He was a little more pleasant. I was so glad I didn't have to take care of him. Throughout my career, when I had a difficult patient, I always tried to be pleasant but firm, especially when the complaint centered on pain medications. I can only give the patient what the doctor ordered for them. When I later worked as a supervisor, I spoke with many such patients, as they often demanded to speak to "the supervisor."

A year after moving to California, I was pregnant again. Our apartment was too small, and Art and I decided to rent a house. We chose a house in Arleta, a small community a couple miles from the hospital. Our house was on a cul-de-sac, with each yard delineated by wooden fencing. Our little house had three orange trees, one of which was very fruitful. My children would pick the oranges, and I would squeeze the fruit for juice. We had a corner lot, with a concrete court on the side, and a tether ball pole. My daughters drew hop scotch squares with chalk and played with the neighbor kids. They rode up and down the dead-end street on their banana seat bikes. My son pulled his red wagon around and rode his Big Wheel. There was a park two blocks away where the kids liked to play. I had my fourth child, Randy, in 1968. I took six weeks off from work, and went back to the night shift.

Art continued working full-time days, while I worked full-time nights. We did make time to enjoy together what California had to offer. We took the children to Disneyland, Knottsberry Farm, and Busch Gardens. To this day, my children still tease me that my favorite ride at Disneyland was "It's a Small World." I loved that ride. We took trips to the beach, watched the Dodgers play, and enjoyed the local parks. We went to Pasadena to view the floats that had been in the Rose Parade the day prior. We went to Grand Olympic Auditorium to watch boxing. I was not a big fan of the sport; this was Art's choice. Nonetheless, I found myself rooting for certain boxers. I remember cheering for Indian Red Lopez. We took a vacation at Palm Springs and another in Las Vegas. Art and I occasionally went out to dinner by ourselves. My daughters' favorite babysitter led the kids in singalongs to Elvis and Beach Boys 45s. We had become true transplants to California.

My job was going well, when an ethical issue involving a fellow nurse cropped up. One night I was working with the charge nurse, when she instructed me to make sure I locked the med cart anytime I worked with a particular nurse. At that time, we did not habitually lock the med cart. I said I would, and the next night I worked with the named nurse, I locked the med cart. There was only one set of keys, and since I was giving medicines that shift, I had the keys. The other nurse approached me and suggested I check on a patient at the other end of the hall. I obliged. When I returned, she was very angry. She picked up a book off the desk and threw it harshly across the desk. She did not tell me why she was angry, but I knew. In my mind, I went through memories of my prior shifts with this nurse. I recalled several times that she sent me on errands, and upon my return, told me that a nurse from another floor called for pain medications, because that floor was out. So, she informed me, she sent some of our medications down to them. The wheels were turning; I was working with a nurse who was stealing narcotics. I never actually witnessed her take the medication, but to ensure someone was monitoring the situation, I did give my observations to the charge nurse who had instructed me to lock the cart. I still had to work several other shifts with that nurse before administration could address the situation. These were awkward, as I had to continue to observe her without her being suspicious. This was one task that was necessary, but I found no joy in it. This nurse went on leave for several weeks, before returning to the job. She did not speak about her leave, but I understood that she had been to rehab. I was glad that she seemed to be doing well, but I kept the cart locked.

After I had been working at the hospital for about two and a half years, a friend of mine called with a job offer. She was a nurse I had known in Pennsylvania, who had moved to California before me. She had accepted a position as the Director of Nursing in a new locked psychiatric facility that was being built on the other side of the valley, in a more rural area. She wanted me to be the night supervisor for the facility. Even though caring for psychiatric patients was not my preference and accepting the position would mean a longer commute, I thought it would be nice to work for her. I accepted. To be completely honest, my decision was also influenced by concerns regarding the previous conduct of the nurse with whom I had worked, and how this reflected on the overall care given during our shift.

Because the facility was thirty minutes away, I decided it was time to learn to drive. Up until this time, Art drove me to and from work. I did not think it was fair to have him drive an hour round trip, twice a day, in addition to his commute which was close to one-hour one way. I had taken Driver's Ed in high school, but failed the parallel parking part of the license exam. I was told that I had parked too far from the curb. I had taken the test with the school's large Edsel. My first mistake. Now it was time—*past* due time—to get my license. For my best education, I decided to pay for a professional instructor. I could not picture my impatient husband instructing me in driving on the freeway. This also allowed Art to stay with the children when I took my lessons. I still remember my first time driving on the California freeway. I would have rather spent an entire night shift taking care of psychiatric patients than driven fifteen minutes on the freeway, but I passed my driving exam.

I started working at the psychiatric facility as soon as the building was finished. However, there were no patients the week I started; they were scheduled to arrive the following week. The facility owner wanted staff to be inside on all shifts to make it look like the building was occupied. The first week, there were just two of us on the night shift, myself and a nursing assistant. I can't say this first week was rewarding as a nurse, but I sure enjoyed it. We watched TV and chatted. I read books and embroidered. We did have one assigned task—to turn lights on and off throughout the facility to make it appear that the building was occupied.

I would turn lights on in one wing, and she the other. The first night, I walked down my wing around 11:30 p.m., and turned lights on in about six rooms. Early in the morning, I went to turn them off. I found that I had not remembered correctly the rooms in which I had turned on the lights. Three or four seemed different. The next night, I noticed the same thing. The third night, I decided to write down the room numbers as I turned the lights on. In the morning I took that note with me when I went to turn off the lights. Three or four of the rooms with lights on were different than recorded. I asked the nursing assistant if she had turned on or off any of the lights in my wing. She said, "No, I wasn't even down there." The same weird light change occurred the next night. After the facility had opened, I mentioned this to a nurse aide who was from the local area. He said casually, "Well you know this was built on a cemetery." Great, I thought, not only am I working in a psychiatric facility, one of my least favorite care fields, but I find out it is haunted. This was my first experience in the unexplained, but as I would find out through my long career on hospital night shift, it was far from my last.

While I was the night supervisor, I also served as the nurse on one of the two wings. I had two nursing assistants with me. Our wing housed mostly people with some form of dementia. We also had a couple of patients with brain injuries. The facility was locked for their own protection, so that they would not wander away. The other wing, opened about six months after the first wing, was not for psychiatric or dementia patients but rehab, housing mostly patients with drug and alcohol addictions. I had a licensed practical nurse (LPN) to look after the addiction wing. An LPN has medical training, but not as extensive as an RN. Thus, their scope of practice is more limited. The LPN had one nursing assistant. I checked on the rehab wing each night, but the vast majority of my time was spent in the psychiatric/dementia wing. After I had been there approximately a year, my friend who had offered me the position had to resign due to health conditions. I continued.

It was at this facility that I experienced another very California event. At 6 a.m. on February 9, 1971, the whole building started to shake back and forth. Papers and books were flying everywhere. Medication bottles were thrown from shelves and the glass ones broke. I was at the nurses' station with one of the nursing assistants. We crouched down to avoid getting hit by the unloosed objects. We just experienced one of California's most deadly earthquakes, with its epicenter in the mountains adjacent to the San Fernando Valley. When it stopped, we immediately got up to check on the patients. That's when the first aftershock hit, less than a minute from the initial earthquake. The magnitude of the aftershock seemed just as severe. I was trying to hold on to the railings so I wouldn't fall while I checked the patients. I'll never forget one lady who was weaving down the hall. She said "I must've had too much to drink last night!" I replied "Then maybe you need to go back and lie down." I helped her to her bed.

We were very fortunate that no patients were injured; however, the facility suffered structural damage. We had also lost electricity, but the generators were operating. They kicked in in less than a minute, but it seemed like a long time as we waited in the confusion. Via television, public announcements came in. We were informed to boil water before drinking it. We were not sure how the morning shift would feed the patients breakfast. The new Director of Nursing, who had earlier replaced my friend, arrived approximately 40 minutes after the earthquake. I gave her my report of the damages I had observed. Information regarding other healthcare facilities started coming in. Some had extensive damage, and there were multiple resulting deaths. There were a few young patients in our addiction wing who had been transferred from another facility, and they also were hearing the incoming reports. They were upset and wanted to go to the other facility to check on patients they knew. We did not let them leave, but told them we would keep them apprised of any information we had regarding the other facility. The Director of Nursing let me leave after I had given my damage assessment and the day shift had arrived.

I was glad to find my family safe when I got home. Art met me at the door with a large brown paper bag filled with broken pieces of the beautiful china tea set I had bought when we lived in Germany. Every piece with the exception of the coffee server was broken. And the lid to the coffee pot was cracked. That evening, I didn't care one bit about the china set. It's times like these that you learn that material things are not important.

I went to work the next night. We boiled water for drinking. We had a lot of cleaning up to do. I worked on getting the medicine room back to standard, and documenting what had been lost. On my wing, the three of us were talking about the earthquake and the damage throughout the San Fernando Valley. One of the assistants said that the previous morning she had noticed that the rooster across the road had not crowed as it usually did before 6 a.m. After that, with aftershocks still coming, we always listened to hear that rooster crow. It was now a pleasing sound to hear.

The day after the earthquake, it took me two hours to get home from work. Many roads were closed and traffic had been rerouted. I later found out that in addition to road damage, some freeway interchanges had collapsed. Traffic was bumper to bumper the whole way home. When I got home, I called the Director of Nursing and told her that I would not make it in that night due to the traffic situation and she should find some-one who lived on that side of the valley. Within a few weeks, our facility, which fared better than many in the area, was back to normal operations.

A few months later, however, I was starting to feel impatient when working with the patients. This was the same feeling I had at the end of my serve at Woodville. I was kind to the patients, but I knew it was time to move on. I saw an ad for an RN on the night shift at Kaiser Hospital, 11 p.m. to 7 a.m. While I would have loved to change to a day or evening shift, night shift was the only one that would work for me with young children at home and my husband working days. I applied and was accepted right away. I felt fortunate, because Kaiser had a reputation for low turnover and therefore few open positions. I gave my two-week notice at the psychiatric facility. Driving away after my last shift, I knew I would never work at a psychiatric facility again . . . although I was once later tempted.

When I started at Kaiser, the hospital was still recovering from the earthquake. I worked on a med-surg unit on the fifth floor. Half of the unit was closed, however, because it was under repair from earthquake damage. Labor and delivery was also on the fifth floor; however the maternity and nursery were on the tenth floor. Several of the RNs who had been there when the earthquake hit told me that the ten-story building had bent at the fifth floor. The floors above slanted forwarded, no longer in align with floors one through five. They said that people on the upper floors thought they were going to die. The building realigned, and they immediately began evacuating. With the maternity and nursery on the tenth floor, the staff placed mattresses on the stairs, so that the mothers could inch their way down in a sitting position, with babies in their arms. The RNs further told me that IV bottles—glass, at that time—broke, and the nurses had to go into full throttle crisis mode to remove the IVs or find unbroken bottles to use. As they told me their stories, I was grateful that I had not sought out the job earlier and been working at Kaiser instead of the psychiatric facility on February 9th. Much of the damage was still visible when I began my position there.

Usually there were two RNs on the floor, but with half of it closed, I worked alone. The doctors only wanted RNs on the floor. I did not have an LPN or nurse assistant. I had approximately 12 patients on my own. If I needed assistance, I would ask for help from one of the RNs in OB or the night supervisor. However, the patients on my floor were not usually critical. Most were post-op from minor procedures. So, I needed assistance only infrequently. As labor and delivery was on the same floor, I could watch the mothers with their new babies getting on the elevator to go to the tenth floor. It never made sense to me why the maternity rooms were not on the fifth floor, across from labor and delivery. Nonetheless, I liked to watch the mothers with their new babies. It reminded me of my time in OB, my favorite area to work.

It was at Kaiser that I learned how to start IVs. When I had started nursing, IV therapy was not common. And at South Side, the interns started them. Now, I was the sole nurse on my floor, and surgical patients required IVs pre and post operation. So, I had to learn. At first, I used the smallest needle, a "butterfly needle," even when accessing a large and prominent vein. Little did I know then that inserting IVs and IV therapy would become one of my more accomplished skills.

It was also at this hospital that I experienced my first night working the Emergency Room as an RN. On Thanksgiving night, I was told to work the shift in the ER; an ER nurse had called off. There were two sides to the ER—a walk-in side and an ambulance side. Having never worked that ER, I knew neither the established procedures nor the location of supplies. Because I was the only RN on the fifth floor, the supervisor had another RN cover my duties there. I never figured out why they just didn't send that same RN to the ER. Now there were two of us in unfamiliar territories. I was assigned to the walk-in side of the ER. Before the rush came, I started going through the cabinets to see where supplies were. When the patients came in, I interviewed them and completed necessary forms, took vital signs, got the patients into gowns, and informed the doctor of their symptoms. I was getting the hang of this, when I was called to the ambulance side, which was getting slammed. I wanted to be very clear to the RNs that I lacked experience in the ER, but would assist as instructed. I told them, "I have never worked the ER. You need to tell me what to do, and I will do it." They said that was okay; they were just glad I was there. I followed all their directions that night. The ER was extremely busy but I got through it. I was glad to have the experience, but happy when the night was over. And as a nice touch, the administration gave everyone working that night a free turkey dinner. The night supervisor came pushing a cart with the Thanksgiving meals for ER. It lifted our spirits; it's the little things. I had only a few minutes to eat, but eating quickly—which I came to understand as a necessary skill for the medical professionals—was something I had learned at South Side.

Each morning, before I ended my shift, I gave my report to the day shift. The day shift head nurse was very strict. She would listen and then immediately go to the charts in front of each patient's room to see if I had charted the information that I had just orally relayed to the day shift. I can understand a head nurse checking the charting of a new employee, but she did this so frequently, it made me feel that she did not trust my work. I was not a new nurse. This went on for a few months, and then she was assigned to an additional floor. Now with two floors to oversee, she was only present at half of my briefings. I welcomed the partial relief. One morning, she raised my indignation when she criticized my cap. The graduate cap styles from the California schools were different than mine. They were more similar to my student cap than my more complicated graduate cap. The head nurse told me, "I don't like how your cap is folded." I felt like I was a student again! But I had a little more leeway in my response now. I simply but firmly replied, *"That's the way it's supposed to be."* That was the end of the conversation. I was proud to wear my South Side cap.

I had become content with my routine. My commute to Kaiser was only ten minutes, and I was comfortable with my duties there. I had been there a year when we decided to move back to Pennsylvania. We had been renting the same house for four years, when the owner decided to sell it. He gave us the option to buy it before he would put it on the market. Art and I had not talked long about whether to buy the house, when Art simply asked me if I wanted to move back to Pennsylvania. I was surprised; from his tone I could tell that he was deferring to me on this significant decision. I immediately said yes. I missed friends and family, and wanted my children to be able to spend time with their grandparents. I was also concerned with my children's exposure to illegal drugs, as this was becoming prevalent in our neighborhood.

When I turned in my resignation to Kaiser, I received another surprise. The head nurse (the one who didn't like my cap) said she would miss me. She further said that if I ever came back to California, she would hire me back.

I received a lot of experience working in California and had some great adventures, but I was ready to head back East. In late spring of 1972, we packed our station wagon. Before we drove off, I took one last look at our small ranch-style house, oranges hanging on the front-yard tree, and the faded-looking mountains in the background. Time for the next chapter in my life.

# CHAPTER 7

# *Home to Canonsburg*

After five years of driving the wide flat roads in the San Fernando Valley, it seemed the streets of southwestern Pennsylvania had grown narrower and steeper. Yet, driving up the brick road to my parent's house, I knew that I was back in the town where I belonged. I loved sitting out on the large porch, chatting with my parents and watching people go by. It was 1972, and in my five years away from Canonsburg, I had not taken one trip back. The old town had not changed much. It was wonderful to walk downtown and see old friends. When someone called my name, a happiness bubbled up in me to be recognized in a place I loved. I loved walking Pike Street, the main street through town, which had many stores I liked to frequent—bakeries, clothing stores, furniture stores, grocery stores, meat markets, and a five and dime store. Art and I enrolled the three older children in a school a few blocks away—first, third, and fifth grades. We decided to stay with my parents for the school year and then look for a house to buy.

Within my first week back, I reapplied for a staff nurse position at Canonsburg Hospital. Because both my parents were still working and Art worked full-time days, I still needed a night shift. At my interview, the Director of Nursing offered me a full-time night shift position on a med-surg floor. I started the following week. On my first night, I felt comfortable as I walked in the front door and saw a lot of the staff, some whom I had worked with before. The nurse I would be working directly with had performed her Woodville serve at the same time I did. They greeted me warmly. The night staff always met in the lobby and talked until it was time to clock in. On the floor, the staff retrieved their caps from their lockers. It felt good to see the recognizable caps from the Pennsylvania schools. I was home.

There had been some changes at the hospital since I last worked there in 1967. The med-surg floors were no longer gender-specific. Both the third and fourth floors had male and female patients, as did the second floor. Further, there were two new units—intensive care unit (ICU) and a telemetry unit. The intensive care unit had five beds, and was equipped with new medical technology including heart monitors. There was an oxygen tank at each bed side. Prior to the establishment of an ICU, patients needing critical care would be transferred to a larger hospital in Pittsburgh. The telemetry unit was an eight-bed unit designed to monitor patients who were not critical enough to need ICU but required continuous monitoring. Prior to the establishment of the telemetry unit, these patients would have been cared for on a med-surg unit.

In addition to these new units, there were new techniques to learn. The most significant was CPR. As a student nurse, I had heard of this technique, but it was neither taught to the nurses nor widely accepted. Now, in 1972, it was a standard procedure. So, I took the first basic life support class that I could. Nurses are required to periodically certify, and the technique has improved over the years. For example, there have been changes in compression to breath ratio. I performed many CPRs in my career, often with advanced techniques such as IV medications and a defibrillator. It is an uplifting feeling when you see the heartbeat appear on the monitor. Your whole being floods with relief and awe.

During the night shift, there were two nurses and two assistants on each med-surg floor, a nurse in ICU, and a nurse in telemetry. There was no staff assigned solely to ER, and the hospital doors were locked at night. We had no security staff at that time. When a patient presented to the ER, the night supervisor would respond. We usually did not receive advance notice that a patient was being transported to our ER; we did not have an ambulance transmitter radio. Occasionally, we received calls via the switchboard from local firemen, who served as first responders, informing us they were on their way with a patient. When someone else, a family member or friend, brought in the patient, he or she rang a buzzer at the hospital doors near the ER. The switchboard operator then paged the supervisor, who went to ER and opened the door. There was always a doctor in the facility; the hospital doctors took turns staying overnight, sleeping in a room on the second floor. Sometimes, this duty was filled by a doctor from another hospital. The supervisor woke the doctor whenever he was needed. The hospital did not receive many ER patients at night, approximately two or three a shift.

I worked the fourth floor, med-surg. I took care of half of the floor. If the floor was full, I would have 15 or 16 patients, and my main responsibility was providing them medications and treatments. Every two hours, the nursing assistant and I made rounds and repositioned any patients who could not turn themselves. In the nurse's notes, I charted the medications and treatments given, the general condition of the patients, whether they had slept, whether they were in pain, and their responses to medications. If one nurse needed assistance with a patient, the other helped.

The camaraderie was high on the night shift. When the shift was over, many of the staff met for breakfast in the hospital's cafeteria, named "Perry Como Dining Room" in honor of one of the town's favorite sons. We would put tables together so we could all talk in a group. The breakfasts were made from scratch—pancakes, egg dishes, pastries. We very seldom talked shop. We talked about our activities, our families, mainly our personal lives. I looked forward to this time together. It was a perfect release after the stress of our nursing duties.

Shortly after I had resumed my nursing career at Canonsburg, I had one particularly satisfying moment. I was at the nurses' station, completing my charting. The elevator next to the desk opened, and a gentleman exited and approached the desk. I could see he was a priest. They often came to visit patients. As he turned to me, I recognized him as the priest who had previously provided the church's required pre-marital guidance. At that moment I recalled his instruction that as a wife, I should not work outside the home. I could tell he recognized me too. While he was cordial, I could clearly tell from the expression on his face that he was surprised to see me there and did not approve. I was likewise cordial. I found the encounter amusing. That was the last time I ever saw him.

It was satisfying to be both back in Canonsburg and working in the profession I enjoyed. Providing care to patients allowed me to assist in their recovery, make them comfortable during their stay at the hospital, and, in some cases, help them to die with dignity. While at a young age, I had desired to be a teacher, looking back years later from retirement, I feel that nursing was my true calling. In a way, it has many aspects of teaching. I particularly enjoyed explaining procedures to patients, providing them care instructions, and answering any questions they had. If I could have changed anything about the job, it would simply have been the shift. But in the early 70's, with Art working days, I did not have that flexibility.

With four children at home, my sleep schedule was divided into two three-hour sessions. The first came after I had walked my youngest to afternoon kindergarten and returned home, and the second after the family had eaten dinner together. On my days off, I slept during the night. While some people are geared to night shift, others never adjust. For the latter, performing night shift can adversely affect their health. As can be expected, a lot of caffeine flows on the night shift. Over the years, I became adjusted to these non-normal sleep patterns. Even after I retired, it took a year before I was sleeping five or six hours in a night.

~ ~ ~

A year after Art and I had returned to Canonsburg, we bought a house a mile from my parents and only two miles from the hospital. Soon thereafter, I became pregnant with my fifth child. It occurred to me that every time Art and I moved, we marked the move with a new family member. I continued working the med-surg floor on night shift until a couple weeks before my due date. While my son Bob had been born at Canonsburg Hospital eight years prior, I delivered my son Allen at the hospital in Washington, Pennsylvania, just a few miles away. Canonsburg Hospital no longer had an obstetrics unit. The state regulators had eliminated the smaller obstetric units when there was a larger unit close by. I was disappointed to see obstetrics go, as it was my favorite unit in the hospital.

Before I delivered my fifth child, I had made the determination that this would be my last child. After this child's birth, I would have five children from ages newborn to twelve. I felt my child bearing callings were more than fulfilled, and I strongly desired to continue to care for patients as a nurse. Plus, we needed my paycheck to make ends meet. So, I arranged for a permanent solution with a tubal ligation. I discussed this with Art. The procedure would be performed the day after the delivery.

In the hospital, everything was going as expected until the doctor presented Art with the paperwork for the tubal ligation. Even though it was hospital policy at that time to obtain the husband's permission, I was upset. I felt that I, a fully competent adult, should be legally able to make the decision for this procedure on my body. Art was given the paperwork, and refused. It was bad timing for everyone. I was in labor—my fifth, as I mentioned—and in no mood for his obstinance. The doctor left, and the argument began. I did most of the talking. I think I wore Art down, because he finally agreed. Before I was transferred to the delivery room, he had signed the paperwork, indicating his permission. After Allen was born, I took maternity leave for a couple of months. It was wonderful to spend this family time together. Soon I was back caring for patients, another aspect of my life that I loved.

~ ~ ~

After working as a med-surg staff nurse for almost three years, I was trained to be a back-up supervisor. It was 1975. The full-time supervisor had some health issues and would require days off with short notice. A major part of the training was the procedure for the emergency room, which at that time was covered by the supervisor. Upon notification from the switchboard operator, I would go to the ER and open the hospital door. As I walked the patient and accompanying persons to the ER, I inquired as to the medical issue. I would then complete the necessary paperwork, call and wake the doctor, and request that he come to the ER. I would stay and assist the doctor. I administered medication, started IVs, wrapped limbs, and performed other procedures an RN would do. If the patient had to be admitted, I initiated the process, which required completion of paperwork. I never knew what to expect when the overhead page announced, "Supervisor to the ER."

During this time, my career was also expanding in another direction. I was asked to help with education, which primarily entailed updating staff on policies and procedures. While the hospital employed a full-time Director of Education, the Director of Nursing desired assistance in educating the off-shifts, i.e. the evening and night shifts. This was because the hospital had to pay overtime when the off-shift staff attended the required classes during daytime. Further, the off-shift staff had complained; they did not like having to attend a daytime class, which often interfered with their normal off-duty routines, including sleep schedules. When the Director of Nursing called me into her office to discuss this opportunity, I had no idea why I was being summoned.

I thought perhaps I had done something wrong. When she offered me the additional teaching duties, I was pleased and readily accepted. I had always wanted to teach, from my early school days when I pretended to teach my class of dolls and stuffed animals.

I started teaching nurses and/or aides, depending on the topic, two to three days a week. On the days I performed the education role, my shift was 7:00 p.m. to 3:00 a.m. This spanned both the evening and the night shift. I enjoyed this shift, as I got to sleep three hours during the night after I came home, before the children were up for school. On the other two or three nights in my schedule, I worked my normal night shift, either on the med-surg floor or, when needed, as acting supervisor.

For each teaching topic, the Director of Education provided me the material. It was up to me to determine the best delivery method. I often combined traditional classroom work with practical application. This was how I was taught in South Side. For example, I wrote a class for nursing assistants in the proper way to take vital signs. We didn't have machines to take them in those days. The class was taught in two parts, over two days. The first was a classroom session. I began with a lecture on the importance of accurately reading and recording temperature, pulse, respiration and blood pressure. I spoke about what specific ranges may indicate and how a doctor may adjust medication based on the vital sign readings. On the second day, I held a hands-on session. The attendees had to take each other's vital signs while I observed them. Then I would check the vital signs myself to confirm they had done it correctly. I would sign off the aides when I was satisfied they could correctly perform the procedure. I observed that one aide did not accurately take blood pressure. At that time, this was performed using a blood pressure cuff and a stethoscope. The pressure cuff was applied to the upper arm, and the aide pumped up the pressure. With the end of the stethoscope in the patient's inner elbow, the aide listened for a pulse as she slowly released the pressure. The first beat heard represents the systolic number and the last beat heard represents the diastolic number. When I questioned the aide, she admitted to being hard of hearing. I had concerns that she was guessing at the numbers, since the numbers were not accurate according to my own results. I did not sign her off on this procedure. I did sign her off on the other procedures. While she could take the other vital signs, another aide would have to take the blood pressure reading.

After I had been teaching for a year, the position for full-time supervisor opened up. Even though I had performed supervisor's duties on occasion when a back-up was needed, I decided not to apply since I was truly enjoying my teaching shifts. In fact, I enjoyed teaching as much as nursing, and was grateful I could do both at the hospital. It was the perfect combination for me, professionally. One morning, after a night shift, I was preparing to leave when the Director of Nursing called me to her office. She said, "I have not received your application for the full-time supervisor position." I told her that I had decided not to apply, because I was now doing the off-shift teaching work. She replied firmly, "I want your application on my desk by tomorrow morning." With mixed feelings, I prepared my application and left it on her desk when I went to work the following night. I did not tell my co-workers, since I had already informed them I was not going to apply. A few days later, I was again called to the Director of Nursing's office. She offered me the job. Thus, started my 40 years as supervisor! It was 1977.

# CHAPTER 8

# *Supervisor*

It was February 1977, when I began my first night as a full-time supervisor. I was in my first-floor office completing paperwork at the beginning of the shift. I took extra care to make sure my cap looked crisp. I was a bit nervous. I knew I was in charge not of a just floor, but of the hospital now. And I had to cover ER; there was nobody else trained for that unit. I was hoping everything would go smoothly. Then I heard Canonsburg's fire whistle blow. That meant one of two things—a fire or a cardiac arrest. At that time, the fire department went to all cardiac arrests. Their rescue truck was equipped with a defibrillator. The little calmness I had that first night left me; I knew ER was my responsibility now. So, I went to the front desk and asked the switchboard operator to call dispatch and find out what the alarm was for. As I waited, I mentally went through the staffing that night, and considered who could assist me in the ER, under my directions. I was relieved when the switchboard operator looked up and said, "It's a fire."

My transition to supervisor was not without some awkwardness. I was now supervising staff that the previous week were my co-workers. I had yet to earn their respect as a supervisor. Further, I had informed them—truthfully at the time—that I was not planning to apply for the position. Thus, I became aware that some of the staff thought I had gone behind their backs and took the job that they anticipated was going to be offered to another nurse. I had my work cut out for me. Initially, the staff was no longer friendly to me, just all business. No one invited me to tea break, as they had done in the past. No one chatted about their personal lives with me. They told me only what was required by the job. I felt that this sharp change was not out of respect for my new supervisor position, but a coolness due to the perceived manner in which I obtained it. I never told the staff, however, that the Director of Nursing had requested my application at the eleventh hour.

When she had offered me the position, the Director of Nursing told me that she had wanted me for the supervisor position because she observed that other staff looked to me for answers and listened to what I said. She said the staff respected me. I appreciated her faith in me and wanted to prove her right. So, when the staff initially was cool to me, I asked her for advice. She simply said, "Give them time. They'll come around." I was grateful for her advice, and I gradually discovered she was right. As a supervisor, I wanted a mutually respectful relationship. I wanted to be friendly but maintain a professional relationship, such that the staff was comfortable coming to me with issues. I wanted the staff to desire to work for me and meet my expectations of high-quality nursing care. I also wanted to excel myself and be a model for the staff. In assuming my supervisory duties, I recalled the instructors and supervisors that had made a lasting impression on me, those that motivated me to want to perform my best. High on this list was my first clinical instructor at South Side. I always remembered her gentle caring nature and effective communication. Also, the compassion and nursing skills of my OB serve instructor continued to influence me.

My daily activity as a hospital supervisor covered both staffing issues and patient care. At the beginning of my shift I would get the report from the 3-to-11 supervisor. There was one supervisors' office, shared between the shift supervisors, as well as the Assistant Director of

Nursing. The 3-to-11 supervisor would be in the office at shift change. She would hand me a written report and then verbally go over it with me. She would inform me how many patients there were and if any were critical. She would inform me of any non-routine occurrences, such as an emergency surgery. She would further inform me of staffing issues, whether any of my nursing staff had called off that night, and who would be filling in, if anyone. After the report, the 3-to-11 supervisor would hand me the supervisor keys, sometimes with the flourish, "Your keys to the kingdom." These keys provided access to all departments as well as supply. This report usually took half an hour.

I usually spent the next half hour completing required paperwork, checking staffing for the day shift, and reviewing policies. I would usually begin my first rounds about midnight. I went to each of the nursing units of the hospital and talked to the nurses. By this time, they had received their units' shift change reports, and had begun rounds. They would inform me of any critical patients or patients with significant problems or complaints. I would visit these patients, along with as many other patients as duties permitted. People who do not work night shift may be surprised, but a large percentage of patients are awake during the night. I would introduce myself and talk to them. In the 1970s at our hospital, many patients were staying overnight for what today would be an out-patient procedure. For example, if a patient needed a gallbladder test, he or she would be admitted the day before. For most of the patients in this category, little care was required. We would ensure they were comfortable and answer any questions they had regarding their upcoming tests.

As the night supervisor, I also spoke with family members of patients. On the night shift, family members were usually only present with ER and critical patients. When a patient died, it was my responsibility to speak to the family. When we were working on an ER or critical patient, I periodically updated the family. I tried to be comforting and understanding yet honest regarding the patient's condition. In providing information, however, I varied my approach, depending on the emotional state of the family members. For example, if the family was strong in handling the crisis and could appreciate knowing that the patient was unlikely to survive, I would share with them the doctor's prognosis. For other families, I may only state that the patient was critical, we were continuing to work on him, and I would keep them updated.

There were other duties that fell to the supervisor. If a nurse needed supplies that were not on her floor, I would go to central supply and obtain them. It could be anything from additional linens to catheters. Another part of my duties was starting IVs. At that time, our hospital nurses were not trained in this procedure and we did not have an IV team. So, when a nurse needed an IV started, I would be informed. There were not many IVs requested during that time period, as antibiotics and pain medications were given by injections, but my IV skills had advanced a long way from my days in California.

As night supervisor, I was a resource to the nurses if assistance was needed. For example, if a nurse had difficulties inserting a catheter or NG (nasogastric tube), I would assist. I also was the only nurse trained in ER, which could take up a significant portion of my duties in a night. Additionally, I had to make sure there was adequate staffing for the next shift. If someone called off, I would call another nurse to replace her, if I felt it was necessary. Back then, we usually had ample staffing.

With this full range of duties, however, I never had to worry about the quality of care the patients received. The nurses on our shift gave excellent care to their patients which made my job easier. I received many compliments from patients regarding the care rendered at our hospital. And several months after I began supervising, the hospital obtained an ambulance transmitter radio in the ER and hired ER staff for all shifts, even night shift. So, there was now one nurse in the ER.

During my shift, I did rounds at least three times. At the beginning, middle, and end of the shift. I usually started on the third floor, starting with ICU, followed by telemetry, and then the two med-surg wings. I then proceeded to the fourth floor (two med-surg wings), followed by the second floor (two med-surg wings), and finally the ER. However, I would revise this routine by starting in any unit that had patients experiencing significant problems. If I had worn a pedometer back then, I would have tracked many miles.

This significant increase in walking on the hard floors, however, did take a toll. About six months into my supervisory duties, I started having pain in my right calve. I initially ignored it. Yes, I was one of those health-care providers who wait to seek medical attention for their own early symptoms. The pain increased, and it became difficult to walk. I decided it was time to get a diagnosis. I did and was informed that I had phlebitis, basically inflammation of the veins in my leg. I was prescribed medication, warm compresses and bed rest. It was too early in my new duties for this issue. While I took a couple weeks of medical leave, I—perhaps unwisely—broke prescribed bed rest to attend a mandatory management meeting during the day. I sat at the end of table with my leg elevated on a chair next to me. I was concerned that if I didn't attend the meeting, I might lose my supervisor job. The condition improved and I returned to work. However, I decreased my walking, and when I worked at my desk, I propped my leg up. I also began wearing support hose. These seemed to help, and I wore support hose the rest of my career.

After a couple weeks off, it was good to be back in my office, putting on my cap and lab coat to start my rounds. In the left pocket of my lab coat, I placed the hospital keys. In my right pocket, I carried my bandage scissors, my hemostat (a tool used to clamp tubing), and a holder of pens of different colors. Each shift used a different color for the nurses' notes in order to easily distinguish the shift that performed the documented treatment. Night shift used red ink. This color distinction only applied to the nurses' notes. Black or blue ink was used for other aspects of the patient's chart, such as requisitions for lab work or x-ray, or transferring doctor's orders to the cardex. The color distinction for nurses' notes was not unique to Canonsburg Hospital; I had been taught this system in my

South Side training. Finally, also in my lab coat pocket, I always carried breath mints, usually Tic Tacs. I now felt adequately outfitted. As I left my office to begin rounds each night, I never knew what my nights would bring.

One morning around 5:30 a.m., shortly after becoming a full-time supervisor, I heard over the intercom, "Supervisor call switchboard." The switchboard operator sat at a desk in a semi-open area with a view of the front lobby. The front doors opened at 5:00 a.m. When I called the switchboard operator, she said, "There is a little old lady in a night gown walking around the lobby." I said I'd be right there. When I arrived in the lobby, I saw an elderly woman in a light ankle-length night gown and slippers. She was pacing the lobby. She did not appear to be one of our patients. However, some patients do prefer to bring their own pajamas. So, I looked for a hospital identification band. She had none. I approached her. "Hi. I'm Ruth, the supervisor. Can I help you?" I was not expecting the response I received. "I need a brain transplant, now." I gently informed her that we did not do that procedure at the hospital. She replied, "But I need one. And I want one." I asked her name, and she would not or could not provide an answer. I asked her where she lived. She simply pointed outside and said, "Out there." She proceeded to inform me multiple times that she wanted the brain transplant right then. I wanted to help her by connecting her back to her family or caregiver. I determined the best course of action was to let the police handle the situation. I decided to take her to the ER, where staff could watch her until the police arrived. I did not want her to be frightened or upset, so I talked to her very gently as I assisted her to the ER. The ER contacted the police. It turned out the police knew who she was and would see that she got home.

On another night, the ambulance brought in a man in his early sixties who was in a cardiac arrest. I had been notified prior to his arrival and was waiting at the ER, as the paramedics brought him in. Six to eight family members arrived immediately thereafter. I escorted them to the waiting room and told them that I would be back to talk to them. I returned to the patient to assist the medical staff. The doctor had intubated the patient, i.e. inserted an endotracheal tube ("endo tube") in the mouth so that the lungs could be inflated with oxygen. I did compressions, while a respiratory tech was "bagging" the patient. She filled the patient's lungs with oxygen by squeezing an ambu bag connected to the endo tube. The other nurse gave medications per doctor's orders. We worked until the doctor called it. There was nothing else we could do.

As supervisor, it was my duty to inform the family that the patient could not be revived, and to escort the family back to the ER, where they could see their loved one and the doctor would answer their questions. Before I left to bring the family back, we removed the ambu bag and other equipment, and ensured the patient looked dignified, i.e. washed blood and other liquids away, placed a clean sheet on the patient, and dimmed the lights. We had to leave in the endo tube; it could not be removed until an appropriate doctor indicated he would sign the death certificate. At that time, this was usually the patient's family doctor or, on occasion, a coroner. The ER doctor could certify that he pronounced the patient dead, but could not sign a death certification that listed the cause of death. I would always tell the family about the endo tube so that they would be prepared when they saw their loved one.

After we cleaned the patient, I went to the waiting room and explained to the family that he had not survived. Naturally, they were distraught. I escorted them to the ER to see the body, and I stayed with them as they spoke to the doctor. Given the number of family present, I thought they may want a quiet place to speak. I told them I would take them down the hall to the chapel where they could talk in private. As we walked, I spoke with some of the family members. Half way down the hallway, a high heeled shoe came flying past my head, missing me by about half an inch. I could feel the air moving as the shoe flew past me. I turned around and found out it was the wife who had thrown it. She was mad and decided to take her anger out on me. No family member addressed this act with her or offered an apology. Someone simply picked up the shoe without word and handed it back to her. Since we didn't have security at that time, I was left to deal with her myself. I decided to, like the family members, refrain from addressing the conduct. I continued as if it had not happened. I opened the chapel door, and informed the family they could stay as long as they wanted, and they needed to call a funeral home of their choice.

Everyone reacts differently to traumatic circumstances. As a supervisor I had to learn how to handle these different situations—mainly by staying calm and talking to the person as I would want to have someone talk to me. However, I will add, that I was grateful when the hospital hired security, lacking my first few years as a supervisor. I fully understand a family's grief, and have been there myself, but in no way is it acceptable to take out their grief by physically harming hospital staff.

After a death, it often fell to me to contact a patient's family members as well as professionals outside the hospital staff. This could be challenging, especially in the era before cell phones. On one occasion in the late 70s, a man came to the ER. He appeared to be in his thirties and was very upset. He said, "There is a sick lady in the bed of my truck. I need someone to look at her." He explained that he was from rural West Virginia and had agreed to drive an elderly couple to Ohio so they could attend a relative's funeral. He was not related to the couple. He had placed bedding in the bed of his truck for the couple, so they could rest during the night drive. While he was driving, the husband communicated to him that his wife was sick. The man pulled off the interstate and followed the blue-H hospital signs to our hospital. After he spoke, the ER nurse went out to the truck. She returned and explained that the woman was dead and a stretcher would be needed to bring her in. The doctor assisted and brought the woman in. Resuscitation efforts were made but unsuccessfully. The elderly man was waiting in the ER waiting room. I went out and informed them that the woman did not survive. The elderly man was visibly shaken. I spoke to him to comfort him and told him I would help him notify his family.

He said his son did not have a phone. When they needed to make a phone call, they used the phone of a particular neighbor, but he did not have her number. I spoke to the driver; he explained he did not know the family. With the name of the neighbor, I called information to obtain her phone number. Eventually, I spoke to the neighbor, informed her there was an emergency and I needed to talk to the elderly man's son. I asked if she could bring him to her house to use her phone to call us back. I left the ER's number with her. About 15-20 minutes later, the son called back. I do not like giving the tragic news over the phone, but I had no choice. I explained the situation and let him speak with his father.

The next step was the issue of transporting the body. A signed death certificate was needed to transport the body back to West Virginia. The ER doctor could not complete the certificate with the cause of death; this is up to the family doctor or a coroner. We called the county coroner. He arranged for the body to be transported to him. Transportation across state lines is usually done funeral home to funeral home, after the death certificate is signed. Understandably, the average citizen is not aware of these legal aspects of death, including transporting the body. This only creates more stress for the family members in the wake of a tragedy. The hospital staff often is left in a position to explain these laws to the family. It took hours to make proper arrangements, which were not completed until after my shift. Before I left, however, the kind driver had offered to take the elderly man wherever he needed to go.

As my experience increased, I became more comfortable navigating each unique situation as it arose. In speaking to the patients and family, I tried to place myself in their shoes and speak to them in the manner I would like to be spoken to. There were times, however, that firmness was best. I know I would have handled the shoe incident in a different manner had it occurred later in my career. I would have diplomatically but straight forwardly addressed the incident with the wife.

When I began supervising, the nursing office was on the first floor of the hospital. A few months later, however, this changed. Canonsburg Hospital once had a school of nursing. They stopped taking students in 1958, the year I started at South Side. The old student nurses' residence remained; it was situated uphill from and separate from the hospital. In 1977, the old residence was renovated to expand hospital operations. After the renovations, a glass-enclosed walkway led from the third floor of the hospital to the first floor of the old student residence. The administrative offices, including the supervisors' office were moved to the old student nurses' residence, now designated the annex. The pharmacy, laboratory, autopsy room, and medical records were also moved.

I never felt safe in the annex, as it was an old building and could have easily been broken into. At night, it was just me and a lab tech in the entire building. My office was on the second floor, and the lab was on the first floor. Anyone could watch us walking across the walkway. On several occasions, the lab technician would see someone looking up at the windows from the hillside. The lab tech told me of one occasion that she spoke with an individual she had assumed was staff but turned out not to be. At the beginning of her shift, a man in scrubs appeared on her floor. She did not know who he was, and assumed he was new staff just checking out the annex. He asked her if she was working alone, and if she was afraid to be by herself. She replied, yes, she was working alone, and no, she was not afraid. She then left for the main building, as she had to draw blood for testing. It was later discovered that the Pharmacy had been broken into that night. We did not have security at that time.

After receiving the report from the 3-to-11 supervisor in the annex, I would often take my paperwork and go back to the main hospital building to complete it. I usually took it to the ER, which now had full-time staffing. The ER had a desk shelf where I would complete my paperwork. Often the Canonsburg police would stop in, check on the hospital, and share a cup of coffee in the ER. I was comfortable doing my paperwork in the ER, and I often had to be there anyway, assisting in care.

As supervisor, I found a new place for my cap. Because I had a shared office, I no longer had a locker. I discovered that the lower left drawer of the supervisor's desk was empty. So, I claimed it for my cap. Likewise, the other supervisors had claimed a location in the office for their caps. At the end of each night shift, I would remove my cap and place it in the drawer. Without my cap, I would go downstairs to the cafeteria and join my night crew for breakfast and fellowship.

# CHAPTER 9

## *The Early Years*

It was about 3 a.m., when I phoned the lab tech on duty.

"Hi, this is Ruth. I have a situation for you."

"Mm-hm."

"I have an ambulance driver here with a burnt leg retrieved from a fire. It's on a stretcher."

"What are you talking about?"

"He tells me he was directed to bring the leg to our lab."

"I don't know anything about this!"

"I was not informed beforehand either. It's probably supposed to go to the autopsy room. So, I am sending them over to you with the leg. Let Doctor Ames know about it in the morning."

I was learning to delegate. As supervisor, I had to address a wide range of issues that were not covered in our nursing books. Most of these issues came through the ER door.

Soon after I began supervising, the night shift experienced an increase in ER volume. I informed the Director of Nursing that we needed a lab tech and an x-ray tech on duty at night, not just on call, for faster diagnosis and treatment. She informed me that currently we could only hire one, and in a few months, we may be able to hire the other. My preference was for the lab tech first.

Like the other shifts, the night shift had its share of patients presenting with chest pain, respiratory problems, and anxiety issues. We also had victims of car accidents, with alcohol often a factor. Additionally, we had the other after-the-bar closes emergency issues, such as injured intoxicated brawlers. We all dreaded working New Year's Eve night. When my shift began on December 31st, I found my anticipation starting to rise shortly before one o'clock, like being on the starting line before a race. Between one o'clock and three o'clock was usually the worst. On the few occasions that we did not have a busy New Year's, we felt lucky.

One night in late spring the police stopped by the ER to tell us that there were three motorcycle gangs in the area for the summer, and they had animosity towards each other. The police expected violence and wanted to give us a heads up that we might have a busy summer in the ER. Fortunately, there weren't any serious injuries—a few non-life-threatening stab wounds, facial injuries and contusions. Although they appeared to be dangerous individuals with their leather jackets, chains, and tattoos, most of them were polite to us and didn't give us any trouble. Yet, we all breathed a sigh of relief when autumn came and they headed out to a warmer climate.

At that time, the Canonsburg Hospital had a small ER—just two beds, with two other beds available in the "Endo" (endoscopy) room, if needed. The beds in the Endo room were used primarily for scheduled endoscopies and colonoscopies performed during day shift, and had the necessary equipment to treat any ER patient. We had one nurse assigned to ER, and one doctor on premises. We would wake him if we needed him. Fortunately, we did not have many situations where we had to treat multiple patients at one time. There were additional hospitals that could be utilized in the event of multiple casualties. One night, however, I was informed that ambulances with five people were on their way to Canonsburg Hospital.

I was doing my rounds when I heard the intercom. "Nursing Supervisor to the ER." Taking the stairs, I hurried down to the ER. There were no patients in ER at that time. The ER nurse told me that the ambulance driver called to inform her that he was transporting five men to our ER. He had provided further details to prepare us. The men were coal miners who had suffered carbon monoxide inhalation. They were, however, awake and alert. We had a few minutes to prepare. I called the respiratory therapist and told her we immediately needed oxygen set up for five patients. I told her she would also have to take five arterial gases. I woke the doctor and informed him of the situation. With only four available beds, including those in Endo, I got a stretcher from x-ray and placed it in the ER for a fifth bed. I placed a piece of paper at each bed so we could document each patient's name, necessary medical information, and vital signs, before we could formally register them. The plan was in place when the patients arrived. The miners were soon all in beds, examined by the doctor, and receiving a low level of oxygen. We would not increase the level until we had the results of the arterial gases. The respiratory therapist efficiently took samples of arterial blood from the wrist of each patient. She took the blood to her office to run the tests that would show both oxygen and carbon monoxide levels. When she returned shortly with the results, we adjusted the oxygen levels. We then started the required ER registration paperwork. The men were discharged one by one as their oxygen levels reached normal. They thanked us for our efficiency in treating them. As they did so, I felt proud of the teamwork in the ER that night.

On another night I was called over the intercom, "Supervisor to the ER." When I arrived, I was informed a cardiac arrest patient was being transported to the hospital by ambulance. The ER nurse and I began setting up the equipment. The patient, a petite elderly woman, was soon brought in. She looked familiar to me, but I could not place her. I felt like I should know her, as if we had some kind of connection. When she arrived, she did not have a pulse, and the report from the paramedics was not promising. We started CPR. We never got a pulse, and the doctor eventually called it. It was my responsibility to speak to the family. It was then that I looked at the ambulance record to get the patient's name, and I realized why she looked familiar. We did have a connection, but the intersection of our lives was at the beginning of mine and I never truly knew her. My mother had spoken of her. I knew her three daughters. Two went to my church, and another was a member of the same lodge as my mother and me, the Pythian Sisters. This daughter was waiting in the hospital lobby. She used to joke that we were cousins; her aunt had married my uncle. Even more close to me, her mother—now my patient— had served as the midwife at my birth. I was delivered at home. According to my mother, it was a difficult birth, and the midwife stayed a week to help out. While this was not routine, this woman went the extra mile for my mother, given their tangential family relationship. I appreciated the interconnections of my hometown. When I knew the family, I was more comfortable when I had to speak to them about significant medical situations. And this night, I found myself at the worldly departure of a woman who had a role in my live. She helped usher me into the world. I grew up and chose the nursing profession, and here I was present, working in the ER at the close of her life. Somehow it completed the circle. I was glad that I was the one there to speak to her daughter.

It was in these early years as a supervisor that I made the first significant change to my uniform—pants. I noticed this uniform change first with the ER nurses. Due perhaps to my three years of nursing school, any change to the traditional uniform initially went against my grain. At that time, all the nurses I worked with were women, and I did a double take when I first saw a nurse in pants. It just didn't seem to present the proper image of a nurse to me. Soon, however, the pants were becoming common and were available in the uniform stores where I shopped. I decided to buy a pair. Just *one*, to try it out. I wore it with a white uniform top, one that went with the uniform skirt. The staff noticed the change. When I did my rounds, I received comments from every unit. I quickly discovered the pants were comfortable and more serviceable to work in. I decided to buy more. It truly made sense in my job, especially when working ER. Many times, I had to assist in transferring a patient from a carrier to a bed. Given my height (5' 2"), I had to get on the bed in order to reach the sheet under the patient. Thus, I kneeled on the bed in a skirt while pulling the sheet towards me. This was somewhat awkward in a skirt. Once I started wearing pants regularly, I never bought another nurse's dress or skirt. After a time, almost all our nurses wore pants, and the uniform dresses and skirts were becoming harder to find. At that time in the late 70s, however, we still wore our caps, at least on our night shift in Canonsburg.

Our night shift had solid esprit de corps. If one unit was extremely busy, a nurse in another unit might ask me if she could go assist. We all pitched in, just as we had done in nursing school. The night shift staff was a different breed. Our lives were somewhat backward from everyone else, as if we were out of sync with normal society, but out of sync together. We were a close-knit group. For the most part, the night shift staff identified more strongly as members of their shift than members of their separate units.

In 1979, a new Director of Nursing was brought in to help us get our policies and procedures up to standard prior to the next inspection. She held two classes to teach the new information. Both classes were held in a large meeting room of a local establishment. At the first class, the night shift sat next to each other on one side of the long table. She made a comment regarding our choice of group seating. A week later when we went to the second class, there were name cards at each place around the table. She had completely split the night shift up. We felt we were back in grade school with assigned seats! And why did she feel it was necessary to try to unknit our closeness? We were glad she only stayed a few years. Her name cards became a source of amusement for us. She could not break our camaraderie.

# CHAPTER 10

# *Call Security*

A few months after I became supervisor, a long-running issue explosively came to the forefront. The evening switchboard operator had been attacked at her station. A man, a non-patient, entered the hospital, walked to the business office area and made demands. He then tried to choke the switchboard operator. Fortunately, he ran out after she screamed for help. The police were called. The hospital had no security guards. The incident forced the Board to again debate the issue. The Chairman of the Board won the debate in an innovative way.

His actions were the topic of conversation among the employees the next day. I was informed that he had placed numerous items on the table at the Board meeting—a picture, a diploma, desk items. He had removed these items from offices of the hospital administrative staff. Late the evening prior, he had walked through the hospital and took the items unchallenged. He declared that the hospital needed security.

A couple months later, our first security guards started their duty. There was one guard on night shift, and I was glad to have him there. Before security was hired, the staff had to deal with potentially physical confrontations on our own or call the police. There were many incidents, most often involving patients. There was the time that a patient suffering delirium tremens ("DTs") ran down the stairwell. I followed him down. As I approached, he tried to hit me. He sat on the steps and yelled at me and refused to get up. A responding policeman resolved the situation, bodily assisting him to his room. On another occasion, a patient with an IV in his arm stood on his bed, swinging his IV pole over his head. He was yelling nonsense. It took several staff, but somehow we got the pole out of his hand without anyone getting hurt. Another time, a tall, very muscular woman broke the restraints that had been placed on her when she was having DTs. I was at a nurses' station when we heard someone running towards us. It was an aide, being chased by this Amazon-built woman. She called out for our help. It took four of us to get the patient back to her room and restrain her again.

While calling police was an option, there was a wait time for their arrival. Also, less severe incidents could be better handled by on-location security. The guards were not direct hires, but obtained through a security company. Companies had different policies. The guards we first had were permitted to assist the staff with aggressive patients. Later on, after a change in companies, the guards were not allowed to touch a patient. This limited their ability to assist us. Nonetheless, I was still glad they were there; their presence often seemed to affect patients' actions, making them more apt to behave.

Over the years, I've called security on many occasions. Too often, it was for patients in withdrawals who became confused and violent. The hospital was not the most appropriate facility for these patients, and I was not afraid to make my opinion known. Once it was clear that a patient was an alcoholic that would experience DTs, a specialized rehab facility would be more appropriate to continue treatment. One night, I was assisting another nurse whose patient was in DTs, had gotten out of bed, and was angrily screaming. The nurse brought in a medication to help him calm down, but could not administer it. I heard the screaming and went to the room. I tried to explain to the patient that we were there to help him. He replied, "You are trying to kill me!" He then threatened to kill us. I shouted to the aide in the hallway, "Call security!" Soon we heard over the intercom "Security to Room 206." The guard arrived shortly thereafter. He tried to talk the patient down, explaining that the nurses were there to help. The patient shouted back, "You're the police. Lock them up!" This went back and forth for several minutes, as I went for more staff help. While the patient was distracted talking to the guard, the nurse went behind him and quickly administered an injection to calm him down. We had enough staff in the room to counteract his subsequent resistance. We got him to bed as the medication began to take effect. The patient continued his rant, but in a more subdued manner. I asked the guard if he would stay outside the patient's room until he was calm. All too often, this was a typical scenario with the patients in withdrawal.

I've also called security to help retrieve patients, especially those who run outside. Sometimes patients in a confused state will wander from their rooms. The confusion could be caused by a reaction to a medication, drug and alcohol withdrawals, or simply the diminishing mental acuity of an elderly patient. I've found that these wandering patients rarely take the elevator, always the stairs for some reason. I have seen patients run outside into the night, and have hurried after them. Each time, as I was running out the door, I would call to the switchboard operator, "Call Security!" Security has searched the parking lot and hospital grounds for patients. If the patient could not be found, the security guard would drive down the entrance road in search of the patient. A few patients have been driven back to the hospital by security.

For confused patients, I have also used security assistance in another manner. On several occasions, patients, not understanding the role of the nurses, would attribute some malevolent intent to our actions. This would often occur when we had a doctor's order to restrain the patient. Such patients have demanded to see the police to report the staff's behavior. I would go out and talk to security. Basically, I would tell the guard, "The patient in room 230 wants to talk to the police; I am being reported. Would you play police and accept the report?" The guard would laugh and follow me back. When the uniformed security guard arrived, the patient would complain to him about how we were trying to harm or kill him. The guard would reply, "I'll take care of it. I'll talk to them. You shouldn't have any more trouble from them." The next time we interacted with these patients, they always appeared to have no recollection of the prior interaction.

Not all calls for security stem from a patient issue. I've called security when I saw an unrecognized person opening the rooms to our oxygen supply. I've called security when staff discovered apparent homeless persons sleeping on couches in waiting areas. I've called security for unruly visitors. Security has escorted out visitors who have engaged in loud disruptive family arguments as well as visitors with erratic behavior, apparently due to drug intake.

Aside from dealing with unruly persons, the security guards had other duties, such as directing traffic when the life flight arrived or departed. I additionally appreciated when the guards notified me of potential issues with the facilities. As they did their walk inside and outside, they would sometimes notice things awry, such as leaking pipes, unusual odors, or burners left on in the kitchen. Mainly, however, it was their response to unusual situations that endeared them to the night shift, especially those peculiar situations that often seem to occur on full moon nights. To anyone who says the full moon doesn't have an effect on people's behavior, I would say come join us on night shift at the hospital.

One such night we heard loud howling coming from outside. "Aaaaaa-wooooo! Aaaaaa-wooooo!" The more experienced staff guessed what this was. One of our frequent patients was being seen in the ER. He was an unusual character, and the staff sensed a connection. I requested the security guard to determine the source of the howling. He halfheartedly went out to begin the search. He found the patient's boyfriend in the parking lot howling at the moon. The security guard asked him what he was doing, and he replied, "I am the werewolf." The guard tried to convince him to leave, but he refused. The guard returned and said, "This one's for the police."

# CHAPTER 11

# *The Move*

The department managers and the supervisors left the monthly meeting in disbelief. It was 1979, and I had been at Canonsburg Hospital now for eight continuous years. I wondered where I might work next. I thought, "If this hospital closes, I'll have to start at the bottom and work up again." I questioned the credibility of the state inspection results of our building.

The building had to be inspected every three years by state regulatory authorities. The hospital administration had just informed us of the result of the most recent inspection. The inspector determined that the building would pass inspection this year, but not the next three-year inspection. He claimed it was due to issues with the foundation that could not be repaired. We were all devastated as we didn't want to lose our community hospital.

Due to the inspector's conclusions, we now had a firm deadline to close Canonsburg's only general hospital, a non-profit facility. Yet, even if we had the finances to construct a new facility, we first had to obtain approval from the state. This turned out to be more difficult and politically charged than I had anticipated. When we first applied for a certificate of need to build a new hospital, our application was denied. State authorities felt the other hospitals in the area could handle the patient load. We started a letter writing campaign to the politicians and influential people of the community. Our community sent over 5,000 letters, as well as more than 2,000 Mailgrams to the governor. It was now 1981, and in order to build a new hospital to continue operations uninterrupted, we would need approval within the year. The situation looked bleak.

Some of the staff began considering other jobs. Several nurses accepted positions at Mayview State Hospital, a psychiatric hospital run by the State. They encouraged me to join them. "It's a State job," they reminded me. The possibility of a secure State job with good benefits was appealing. However, I knew from experience that I would not be able to work with psychiatric patients for the rest of my career.

Fortunately for me, we were finally given the go ahead to build a new hospital. I found out the wonderful news at a managers' afternoon meeting. We were elated! To celebrate, after the day shift administrators and managers were finished for the day, we met at a pub. Everyone was happy and positive. Over hors d'oeuvres and drinks, we began our informal planning. We knew we had much more work ahead of us, but were ready for the challenge. Next step—fundraising.

As a nonprofit stand-alone hospital, we had no parent corporation to support us financially. A fundraising campaign was started. We appealed to the residents of Canonsburg and surrounding communities as well as staff members. I pledged a donation via a monthly salary deduction. People were very generous to the cause. The new hospital was becoming a reality. The administration considered various sites, and selected a 31-acre site just a mile from the current hospital. This whole process moved like a fast train, given the time pressure we were under. The ground breaking ceremonies took place August 22, 1981. I had wanted to go, but having worked the night prior, I skipped the morning ceremony. Nonetheless, I was given a small metal shovel commemorating that day.

The goal was to have operations fully running in the new hospital within two years.

Meanwhile, all the managers had to come up with a plan for transitioning their new departments. The supervisors were also given assignments. Being that I oversaw the entire hospital at night, and did not have a specific unit, I wondered what my assignment would be. At the managers' meeting, the Director of Nursing looked at me and said, "You'll be in charge of designing a department for outpatient endoscopies and colonoscopies." My mind went blank, but I dutifully nodded my acknowledgement. I knew very little about these procedures. At that time, these scheduled procedures were performed in a designated ER room during day shift. A gastroenterologist was assisted by the ER staff. Now, we were going to set up and staff an outpatient surgery unit, ambulatory care. I not only had to design the department but I had to determine and order the necessary equipment, set up the rooms, and interview and hire two nurses. I had a lot of research ahead of me.

I began my research by talking to the day shift ER nurses who assisted in the endoscopies and colonoscopies. I asked about the equipment needed and had them walk me through the procedures. I sought their input for a well-designed unit. I also read articles on the procedures. At my request, another hospital graciously took the time to show me their unit. I also visited the under-construction hospital to visualize the area I was designing. The managers and supervisors were permitted to visit the site at a certain point in construction. So, with hard hat on, I was escorted by a construction worker to the area I was responsible for. It was exciting to see the progress throughout the new hospital.

I sketched my design for the outpatient surgery unit. In addition to the surgery rooms, I made sure to include a sufficient-sized supply room and a nurses' station with a desk large enough to hold files and computers. After taking inventory of the ER equipment and the condition of each piece, I went to central supply and asked for a medical equipment catalogue. I selected the equipment I wanted, took my list back to central supply, and requested them to order it. Now for the hiring process. Human Resources had already posted the nurse positions in-house and received applications. If an in-house applicant was not selected, the position would be publicly advertised. I interviewed each applicant, and sent my recommendations to Human Resources. The positions were filled.

The old hospital building was sold. Before we moved into the new building, we found out that the new owners of the old building intended to use it for a skilled nursing facility. This further raised our suspicions as to the motive for the state inspector's earlier determination regarding the foundation. (I discovered that I was not the only one who secretly held such skepticism.) After we had moved out, the old hospital was soon renovated and, indeed, began operating as a skilled nursing facility.

The day before the move, the night shift staff had breakfast together after work. We did not think this would be the end of our ritual. We thought we would continue this routine in the new hospital, but we soon discovered that this would not be the case. Breakfast was not served until 9 a.m. I remember this last breakfast together. Almost all the night staff joined that morning. It was a bittersweet moment. We were happy to be going to a new facility, but we knew we would miss the old hospital. There was a surreal atmosphere as we sat together in the old cafeteria one last time. Somehow, we knew things would not be the same.

The next morning, double staff were on duty—one at the old hospital and one at the new. Most part-time staff were scheduled to work the move. All units and both ERs were fully staffed. The timing of equipment transfer was carefully planned out so that there was adequate equipment for patients at both locations throughout the transfer. Ambulances waited in line outside the ER doors. All available ambulances from surrounding communities were used.

We started getting patients prepared early, during the end of the night shift. Breakfast was served early. A teenage patient was given the honor of being the first patient in the new hospital. He was brought down to the ER and loaded into the first ambulance in line. As that ambulance departed, the next one in line pulled up for the second patient. This went on like clockwork all morning.

I did rounds as usual, but with a different focus. After my official shift was over, I went down to the business office to assist in boxing up paperwork and files. I left for the day around 9 a.m. As I took one last look at the ambulances going up the hill to the new hospital, I had mixed emotions. While it was a bittersweet moment, just knowing that I would be there at the beginning of the healthcare in the new facility, modern and with new equipment, lessened the sadness of leaving the facility that filled so many of my memories.

# CHAPTER 12

# *New Hospital*

"Wow! This is a great ICU." It was my first shift at the new hospital, and I was walking the floors with another supervisor. The new hospital opened on May 14, 1983. For that first night, we had two hospital supervisors on duty, and it was exciting to tour the new hospital with a fellow supervisor. While we had toured the facility before the equipment was in place, it looked completely different now that it was up and running. The place was alive. It was clean, spacious, and well-equipped with new technology. For a career nurse, this was akin to a trip to Disney World.

In the old hospital, the ICU was one large room with five beds divided by curtains, and a nurses' desk with monitors. The new ICU had seven beds, each in its own room with a glass door. At the center of the ICU was the nurses' station new monitors. The patient rooms were situated on the two sides of the nurses' station. Behind the nurses' station was the medicine room, a small kitchen, a small conference room, and a bathroom. The ICU nurses also had their own combination lounge and locker room adjacent to ICU. My fellow supervisor and I were quite impressed. Before we left ICU, we told the nurses we would be back, so they could show us how to work the new monitors.

We proceeded to the ER. We now had a regular ER doctor, one who specialized in emergency medicine. In the old hospital, the doctors took turns covering ER; most of them were family practice doctors. The new ER had five rooms and seven stretchers, which we simply referred to as beds. Three rooms were for specialized care. The trauma room had two beds; the cardiac room had two beds; and the "gyne room" had one bed with stirrups for patients that needed vaginal exams. The two other rooms were for general ER care and had one bed each. While a patient could be treated in any of these ER beds, we specialized if possible, since the corresponding equipment was placed for quick access. For example, a cardiac crash cart was adjacent to the cardiac beds, but it could be wheeled elsewhere if needed. The equipment was new—the beds, the monitors, the radio transmitters, the equipment on the crash carts. It was like opening Christmas presents. A medicine room, doctor's work area, waiting room, doctors' lounge, and nurses' lounge completed the ER.

On the hospital grounds close to the ER was another significant addition—a helipad! In the old hospital, we did not have a helipad. Therefore, when a life flight was either delivering or picking up a patient, the helicopter would land in the parking lot of the nearby high school. During night shift, this meant that I would direct someone to call the fire department, as we needed their spotlights to light the premises before the pilot could land. An ambulance was used to transfer the patient the short distance from the hospital to the helicopter at the high school or vice versa. I had been informed that on a day shift when the school parking lot was full, an area of the hospital parking lot had to be cleared of cars. So, the helipad was a huge positive change for us.

The other supervisor and I continued upstairs to look at each wing. The new hospital had two floors, and with the exception of ICU, all nursing units were on the second floor. The South wing had primarily the surgical patients, pre- and post-op. The West wing contained medical patients, including all telemetry (constantly heart monitored) patients. The telemetry patients were no longer in a separate area. However, the telemetry monitors were in one location at the wing's centralized nurses' station. The North wing was a skilled nursing unit, with an inpatient rehab unit. The skilled nursing unit was a new specialty for Canonsburg Hospital, and a stipulation for the approval of the new hospital.

On the second floor, we made a few wrong turns. The new hospital was larger and more spread out. It took me a few days to become familiar with the layout. One of the administrators anticipated this. He was working the first night, and told us supervisors to call him if we needed to go to central supply. He would walk us down so that we would not get lost.

We continued on our tour of each wing, and were impressed with what we saw. The old hospital contained mostly two-bed and four-bed rooms; there was only one or two private rooms on each floor. The new hospital was the reverse. On West and South wings, the vast majority of rooms were private. There were, however, eight two-bed rooms—four on West and four on South. The North wing, the skilled nursing unit, had two-bed rooms. We were also impressed with the new staff lounge. There were no nurses' lounges at the old hospital. This one had a table and chairs, refrigerator, microwave, and bulletin board with notices of upcoming events or educational items. The lockers and bathroom were adjacent. The lounge was a designated smoking area for the staff.

After we had toured the second floor, we went back downstairs to ambulatory care—the unit I had designed. I was anxious to see how it came out. We went room to room as I checked each detail. I was pleased, nothing was missed in the equipping of the rooms. I was proud that my efforts resulted in the unit before me. I felt I had done this extra duty well.

From there, we went on to x-ray, lab, and medical records. The medical records department was significant to me, because there were no personnel in that department at night. So, if a doctor needed records, I would have to go to the records room and get them. In the old hospital, I did this frequently for ER, and had a long walk to obtain records. From ER, I would walk up to the third floor, across the walkway to the first floor of the annex, then up to the second floor of the annex, and down to the end of the hallway to reach records. Once I found the record, I retraced this path. In the new hospital, records were on the same floor as ER, down one long hallway. A much shorter walk.

Finally, we went to central supply. Central supply consisted of several rooms, including one with two autoclaves for sterilizing equipment. We took some time there trying to familiarize ourselves with the location of various items. Having normal duties that night, we ran out of time to complete the full self-tour.

It wasn't until the next night that I had time to explore the new OR. As I put on booties over my shoes, removed my cap, and put on the OR headcover, I was eager to see the layout and equipment of the new OR. It was amazing. As with the other units, it was larger than we had in the old hospital. The new OR likewise had new up-to-date equipment. The hospital could do more surgeries, as well as more types of surgeries. It was important that I familiarize myself with the items in the OR supply room. It was my responsibility to obtain any items, such as sutures and staples, that the ER lacked for patient treatment during the night.

The supervisors took time arranging our new office. An added bonus was that it was no longer shared with the Assistant Director of Nursing, as in the old hospital; it was a dedicated supervisors' office. It was on the first floor, near the front desk, a short hallway away from the ER. This was fortunate as I was soon spending much of my time in the ER. The office had all new furniture, including a new desk. On my first day, I claimed the bottom left drawer, once again, for my cap.

As I began working in our new impressive hospital, I would have never guessed that in just a few years, we would have to build a larger ER, reduce the nurses' lounge in ICU to accommodate a new bed, and build an ambulatory care unit much larger than the one I had designed.

# CHAPTER 13

## *Patient Increase*

Straight from its opening day, our hospital soon became very popular. Ambulance companies knew of our new ER with its greater capacity, and the ER rapidly increased in patient volume. It also seemed that there were more persons arriving at the ER by family car. Our reputation obviously got out. Our med-surg units also were rapidly near full capacity. Patients and their family members were pleasantly surprised by the private rooms, and expressed their appreciation. I recall a man who had brought his elderly mother to the ER. The doctor decided to admit her to the hospital. When I explained this to the man, he indignantly demanded that she be in a private room. I calmly replied, "Almost all our rooms are private rooms." His expression lightened. "They are?" As a medical provider, I felt the private rooms benefitted the healing process.

However, being so full, we did have to admit patients to the two-bed rooms. As I did rounds, I always carried a clipboard with important documents. I kept the hospital census report on top. This report showed the number of patients in each unit. At that time, it was the supervisor who decided which room the patient would be admitted to, based on the doctor's diagnosis. Often, I would first call the floor and speak to a nurse to know that unit's preference. Sometimes finding a bed was challenging. On occasion a new admission coming from ER would have to stay overnight in the ER until a bed opened on the second floor. On a few occasions, I had an ER patient needing a telemetry bed, and none were available. I did not want to leave the patient on a stretcher in ER; he would be more comfortable in a regular hospital bed. So, I would check with ICU. If they had more than one empty bed (I would not request their last one), I would move the patient to ICU temporarily, until a telemetry bed opened. However, I ensured that the patient was marked telemetry, so he would not be charged for an ICU bed. I would always explain the plan to the family.

On other occasions, all rooms were occupied, but a couple of the two-bed rooms had only one patient. If the newly admitted patient was of the opposite gender, I would have to move single patients into the double rooms together. I always asked the patient first. If they refused, I would not move them. But many patients graciously agreed.

Once, I got a call from ER stating that a patient needed to be admitted, but we had no beds available. Not one. I told the ER nurse that they would have to hold the patient until morning. About an hour later, I was notified of a patient death. After the body was moved to the morgue, I called housekeeping. I told them we need a room cleaned ASAP. The room cleaning requires a complete room wipe down—floors, bathroom, bedframe, nightstand, chair . . . everything. I encouraged them to make this room a priority. An hour later, I called back down to ER. "I have a room now for your patient."

Another factor resulting in the ER and ICU patient increase was that the nursing facility a few hundred yards from the hospital had recently opened a longterm care wing for patients with head injuries. When these patients experienced difficulty in breathing and other medical problems, they would be brought to our hospital. For most of these patients, I would inform the ICU of the incoming patient and condition. Often, I'd say, "He has a trach and is on a vent," meaning the patient had a tracheal tube and was on a ventilator. At that time period, there were not many facilities specializing in head-injured patients on ventilators, and thus, the nearby nursing facility had patients who had been transferred from hospitals near and far. These patients usually required admission for further and advanced treatments not available in the nursing facility. Most could not communicate and required close observation and total care. Several of these patients were admitted on multiple occasions. My staff and I got to know their medical issues as well as their personal stories. We normally were informed of the latter via the patient history provided by the nursing facility and/or visiting family members. Sadly, many of these patients were young adults. In the years shortly after the new hospital opened, there were usually one or two of these patients in ICU on most nights.

Not only was the hospital, with its private rooms, more comfortable for the patients, but it was also quieter. With one exception, we no longer used the intercom system. Managers and supervisors were given pagers. When my pager went off, I was to go to the nearest phone and call the extension appearing on the pager. The ER, however, had two numbers—one for standard pages and one that meant they needed me in the ER stat. The one exception—for which the intercom system was still used—was emergency codes.

I responded to all "codes" wherever they occurred in the hospital. There were several codes—one for cardiac arrests, one for a missing patient, another for a person with a weapon, another for a fire drill, and others. The vast majority of codes that occurred were for cardiac arrests. When the cardiac arrest occurred in any unit other than the ER, a staff member would pick up a phone and dial a 3-digit number that rang the code phone at the front desk. When the switchboard operator answered the code phone, the staff would say "Code Blue" and give the room number. The switchboard operator would then announce it over intercom—"Code Blue; Room ___!"—three times. When we heard the announcement, the ER doctor, the respiratory therapist, and I would hurry to the announced room. When the code occurred in other than the West wing, a West wing nurse would also sometimes assist, as they were trained in reading the monitors. When the code occurred in the ER, it was not announced over the intercom system, but I would be individually paged.

As with all nurses, I was certified in BLS, Basic Life Support. At the new hospital, a policy was implemented requiring nurses to be certified in ACLS, Advanced Cardiac Life Support. Now, in addition to CPR, we had to learn how to conduct a code—to read the monitors, intubate the patient, administer the appropriate medication, and defibrillate. I was given a book to study before the eight-hour class. In class, we reviewed updates in basic life support procedures. Then we were instructed on medications and dosages for cardiac arrests, which varied according to heart rhythm, and the timeframe between medications. We studied the various rhythms as displayed by patterns on a monitor. I had a flashback to 1967 when a fellow nurse and I obtained a book in attempt to teach ourselves the meaning of the patterns. In order to receive our certification, we had to pass a comprehensive test and prove our ability in a practical exercise. We were observed performing an intubation (inserting the endo tube though the mouth to the trachea). At the squeeze of the ambu bag, we listened with a stethoscope for the air to make sure the tube was properly placed. We were observed performing chest compressions and reading monitor strips. We were observed directing a code—reading the monitor, calling out the medications to be given, and directing the code team through the resuscitation process. For this first class in ACLS, the attendees were tested individually in directing the code. This was the most difficult practical test given in the ACLS class. I knew my instructor; he was the ER Director, and understandably very exacting. So, I was a bit nervous as I walked through the door to his testing room. If I did not pass this class, I could not be a supervisor. In his room, I read the monitor, told him the rhythm and what medications I would be giving. I told him, "We are continuing CPR." I felt I was doing well when he changed the rhythm on the monitor. I revised my directions. This repeated several times.

Finally, he said we were done, and I could proceed to the next testing section. It was a draining day, but I was always glad to improve my skills.

ER care kept me busy. For the first 90 minutes of the night shift, there were two RNs in the new ER. This was because one of the evening shift nurses worked 4:00 p.m. to 12:30 a.m. After that, we only had one RN until 7:00 a.m. A secretary was hired just for the ER. This freed the nurse to focus on patient care. Yet, even with the secretary performing administrative work for the ER, the volume of patients was too much for one RN. When an additional RN was needed, I would be paged. Responding, I would hurry down to ER and would ask the ER nurse, "Where do you want me?" At her request, I would start IVs, administer medications, perform EKGs, apply dressings, and provide other care needed. Soon, assisting in the ER was consuming four to six hours of my night. I recalled one night we were very busy, and a male teenage patient tested my tolerance for disrespectful behavior. He was mad because we had not yet discharged him and we were taking care of other patients. These patients were in critical condition and had triage priority. He got off his bed and, standing, loudly swore a blue streak, with "F*** this," over and over. I had had enough. I went over to him, and said, "I've had enough of your mouth! There are other people in this emergency room who don't want to hear you talking like this. I don't take that language from my children, and I will not take it from you. So, sit down and be quiet!" Surprisingly, he complied. ER was too busy for the staffing we currently had. I raised the issue with the Director of Nursing and explained the need for another ER nurse. The administration listened and hired an LPN for the ER night shift. While this was helpful, there were many things the LPN was not permitted to do, such as starting IVs and giving IV medications. So, I still performed a large percent of my shift in the ER.

I also had an additional duty, with the move to the new hospital—administering blood transfusions. This was in addition to my responsibility to start and restart most IVs. In the old hospital, when a patient needed blood, the attending nurse would give the patient the blood. At the new hospital, an IV team was created. This team, rather than the attending nurses, performed all blood transfusions. There was one big exception—night shift. The IV team only operated day and evening shifts. For the night shift, instead of continuing the policy of having the attending nurse perform the procedure once the IV had been inserted, this duty was allocated to the supervisor. When the policy change was implemented, I performed eight to ten procedures a week, on average. The ER and ICU performed their own blood transfusions; I simply obtained the blood for them from the lab tech. For all other patients, I performed the procedure. This entailed going to the laboratory to get the blood, confirming matching data with the patient's information, administering the blood, checking vitals to ensure no adverse reactions, and charting. I would observe the patient for approximately 15 minutes, after which a unit nurse would takeover. My part in this could take an hour. Often during this time, I would be paged to the ER. When that would happen, if I had already hung the blood, I would have a nurse finish the vital signs. If I hadn't hung the blood yet, I would place it in the unit's medicine refrigerator, and start keeping track of time. I had a limited time to begin to administer it, one hour.

My daily walking increased at the new hospital. Out of curiosity, I wore a pedometer several nights. On very slow nights, I might log only three miles. On busy nights, my steps covered five miles. As supervisor, I was often the go-for person when nurses needed supplies, medication, or equipment not on their unit. This meant frequent walks to central supply for additional sutures, catheters, isolation racks, and other items. And there were a few unusual things I was asked to obtain. Once I received a page from the ICU. I answered, and the ICU nurse informed me that a patient was demanding a ham sandwich; she would not eat anything else. Although my inclination was not to respond as if the hospital was a hotel, I nonetheless did not want an ICU patient to become agitated over the food. Not being very busy at that particular moment, I went to the closed kitchen, located all the ingredients, and made her a ham sandwich.

While we were usually quite busy, I was pleased with the new hospital—the private rooms, the dedicated supervisors' office, the larger and state of the art ICU and ER, more specialists, and the general newness and brightness of the building. There was, however, one major disappointment.

The night shift never coalesced the same as in the old hospital. There was more than one reason. First our morning breakfast ritual was not continued, as there was no hot breakfast before 9 a.m. Second, the new staff were not hired for a dedicated shift, but rotated between the shifts—days, evenings and nights. They, thus, identified more closely with the unit they worked on as opposed to a shift. Third, due to the hospital's layout, the units were more separated. While we were all friendly, the magic of the old night shift could not be recaptured.

If I had to go back in time and pick one week to work again, it would be at the old Canonsburg Hospital with the old night shift. I would have a cup of tea with the fourth-floor staff after I made my first rounds. On another round, I would mention to the nurses on the second floor that the third floor was really busy. One of the nurses would say without hesitation, "I'll go help them." I would stay on the second floor until she came back, in case her floor needed assistance while she was gone. After work, most of the staff would go down to the dining room where we would purchase hot breakfasts made fresh for us. We would sit around the long table together and talk and laugh about what was going on in our lives.

# CHAPTER 14

# *The Evacuation*

It was early autumn in the mid-1980s as I drove up the hill to the hospital before my night shift. I slowed to make my turn left for the short road into the employee parking. One of our security guards was standing at the end of the road stopping vehicles. I could not see anything beyond him. I assumed that there was a life flight helicopter landing on the helipad adjacent to the parking lot. Security stopped cars when flights arrived or departed. That was not the reason, however. I rolled down my window, and he said to me. "Go park at the bottom of the visitors' parking lot. PT is up by the front doors. She'll explain everything to you." He was referring to the 3-to-11 hospital supervisor, Patricia Thomas. No one called her by her full name, just "PT." She was both my colleague and my dear friend. On days we both worked, she gave me the verbal supervisor's report. I had known her for years. We both had four children until my son Allen was born in 1974. She joked that I had one-upped her.

As I drove off to the visitors' lot, curiosity raised my alertness a notch. As I turned into the lot, my curiosity changed to concern. Before me, I saw patients and staff throughout the parking lot, with police presence. I quickly found a parking spot, and hurried to the front door, looking for PT. With her signature puffy blond hair, each lock perfectly in place, as if she just walked out of a beauty salon, she was easy to spot. She was standing just outside the front doors, with clipboard in her hand, speaking to one of the nurses. I interrupted, "What's going on?" PT explained that a bomb threat had been called into the hospital's front desk. Upon being informed, PT directed the front desk to contact the police and then called the hospital administrator, whose direction she was now following. This entailed evacuating the patients that could be and having police scan the hospital with bomb-sniffing dogs. With the exception of ER and ICU, all patients had been evacuated, and PT was now waiting for the dogs, which had to be brought in from Pittsburgh. I asked her why she hadn't called me in earlier that evening so I could have helped her. Calm and in charge, she said, "We had enough help." She had called in the relief supervisor, Mary Lou, and assigned her to take charge of evacuating the patients in the North Wing, skilled nursing. PT handled the South and West wings. She walked me through the entire operation, after which she handed me the "keys to the kingdom" along with a clipboard that held a list of all the patients. She said, "I got them out; you can get them back in." PT left for home and I surveyed the scene.

At that time, the hospital did not have an evacuation plan; yet each wing managed to stake out their own area of the parking lot. Given that it was the night shift, the visitors' lot was empty. With ER and ICU remaining in the hospital, it was the second-floor med-surg units in the parking lot. The North wing skilled nursing unit was on their side of the building, near the North side exit door. South and West wings filled the main parking lot, with South in one area and West in the another. The South and West wings each had three teams. Each team was also together, headed by a nurse, in its own claimed space. Some patients were in wheelchairs; some were lying in their beds which had been wheeled into the parking lot; some were in chairs that had been removed from the kitchen, and some chose to stand. Patients had blankets draped over their shoulders. Several IV poles and portable oxygen tanks shined under the parking lot lights. Med carts were sprinkled throughout the lot, one for each team. The carts looked similar to a mechanic's tool box. They contained a separate drawer for each patient with their medications. The bottom drawers contained narcotics. There were approximately 100 patients and 16 attending staff in the parking lot. The night shift is staffed with less nurses and attendants than the day shift or the evening shift. This promised to be a challenging night.

As I looked over the scene, I recalled a year at the old hospital when we had four bomb threats. Each time, the switchboard operator immediately contacted the emergency dispatch, but we did not evacuate. On each of these occasions, the police instructed us to have the staff look around and see if they saw anything unusual. If we did find something unusual, we were to report it to the police. As hospital supervisor, I directed the staff on each unit to check their areas. I took responsibility for checking the areas on the first floor and the annex. We checked all areas, looking behind doors, on shelves, and in waste baskets. If a patient was awake and asked a staff member what he or she was doing, the staff would make up a story, such as looking for some papers they had lost. We did not want to alarm the patients. There had been no evacuation and no police walk through. Times had changed and procedures were different now, both for the hospital and the police.

I put the keys in my pocket and started my "rounds." I went through the parking lot and spoke to each nurse. I asked them how they were doing and if they needed anything. The staff remained calm and upbeat, taking the evacuation in stride. They were continuing patient care, providing medications and comfort measures, and generally keeping a calm demeanor that seemed to rub off on the patients. Most of the patients I spoke with also had similar attitudes as the nurses. They had been told the reason for the evacuation, but were not anxious. Some were waiting to see the dogs arrive. Others however, understandably expressed anger towards the unknown person who had called in the threat. Some asked me when they would be able to go back in. A couple of times, a nurse explained she needed a prescribed medication that was not in the patient's drawer. I went to the other nurses and asked if they had any patient on that medication. The med cart often has, in each patient's drawer, two to three days of medications. I explained we needed to borrow the medication and it would be later replenished from the Pharmacy. I was fortunate on both occasions; we were able to do this.

After I had made the rounds to each area, I noticed the temperature had dropped a few degrees. Even with a blanket, a few of the older patients appeared to be feeling the chill. I asked a police officer if he could call dispatch and see if there were a few ambulances available that we could use to shelter some patients, so they could keep warm until it was declared safe to go back into the hospital. He obliged, and four ambulances arrived. Several of the patients were placed into the back of the ambulances and given extra blankets.

ER staff continued to work in the hospital, but they were not accepting new patients. They worked to discharge patients as expeditiously as safely possible. The ICU continued its care without interruption or change. At the time of the evacuation, there was a doctor in the hospital completing medical records. He volunteered to stay in ICU in case the nurses faced any emergencies.

About 12:30 a.m., the dogs arrived. A murmur of relief arose through the parking lot. "The dogs are here." I introduced myself to the police, as they led two dogs into the building. The dogs had to be walked through each room of the hospital. We waited. An hour or so later, the police exited the building and gave us the "All clear." Now, we just had to get the patients back to their rooms. This turned out more difficult than I expected.

For patient accountability, I had to ensure documentation of each patient's re-entry. I told the North wing to begin bringing in their patients through the North entrance. I informed the nurses to document each patient's return, to offer them a hot drink and an extra blanket. The South and West wings re-entered through the main lobby. With my clipboard in hand, I stood in the lobby and marked off patients one by one as they entered. Given the variations in ambulatory capability, the teams could not enter as a group. The nurses decided who would wait with patients in the parking lot and who would help patients settle in on the floor. An aide wheeled in the patients; some patients walked in on their own. Unfortunately, many patients did not remember their room number. When this first occurred, I thought, "No problem; this information is on the patient band."

When a patient was admitted, the admission office prepared an identification "stamper." The stamper machine created a square metal plate approximately 3 x 3 inches with patient information. This included the patient's name, birthdate, patient ID number, doctor, and room number. This plate accompanied the patient's admission sheet to the unit. The plate was then used to stamp the patient's medical papers—the nurses' notes, doctors' orders, test results, requisitions for lab work or x-rays, and basically any documentation connected with that patient. The stamp was also used to create the patient ID band, worn on the wrist.

The elderly woman stood in front of me, seeking assistance in locating her room. "Let me see your band," I said. She raised her wrist, and I read the information. It was then and only then that I realized the room numbers were not on the name bands. The room number was the last item on the stamper. In order to fit the stamped paper into the plastic wristband, a portion was cut off—the bottom inch with the room number. When I checked the other patients needing assistance, I found that this was a standard practice. I stopped the aides in the lobby and asked them to take these patients to the second floor and assist them in finding their rooms.

It took an hour to ensure all the patients were settled. At that point, I called the on-call administrator and informed her that police had given the all-clear, patients were accounted for, and operations were normal. After the call, I started my normal rounds. I made sure patients were well-cared for, and I thanked the staff for their excellent patient care and attitude throughout the evacuation. The person who called in the bomb threat was never identified. We all wished that the person had been caught. A bomb threat to a hospital unquestionably places many patients at higher risk. To me, an arrest and jail time would have brought some sense of justice.

At the next managers' meeting, I raised the issue of the patient bands lacking room numbers. This led to changes in the stamper. The machine was modified and all information was fit into an area that could be included within the plastic wrist band.

# CHAPTER 15

# *Picnics*

A group of six nurse managers and supervisors met in the hospital dining room to practice. Pixie, the nurse manager of 2-South handed each of us a sheet of paper with the lyrics she had created. To a popular tune of the day, we began, "We are the bosses!" I sang soprano. At the end of the session, we determined we weren't ready; we needed another practice before our upcoming debut. A talent show had been added to the annual hospital picnic, and we decided we could not pass up the opportunity to have some extra fun.

Our hospital picnics started back when we were in the old hospital. It was a way that the hospital could say 'thank you" to the employees for their dedicated work all year long. The first picnic was held at a farm that belonged to a friend of the administrator. The time was set so that all shifts could come at some time during the designated hours. Families were welcome. Food and drinks, including a keg of beer, were provided. The picnics continued after we moved to the new hospital, but because we had more employees, we needed a larger place for the picnics. We rented a pavilion at Washington Park, a city park. At the park, there was a stage with seating around two sides. Perfect for the talent show.

So, for our first talent show performance, the managers and supervisors bought matching blue shirts with "BOSS" printed on the front in big black letters. I can't remember all the words to our song—"We are the bosses!"—but we sang three verses. The audience laughed and clapped. That was the start of our picnic talent show singing group. Each year we enjoyed the pressure on our creative talents, as we tried to come up with another entertaining song. One year, we wore jeans, plaid shirts, boots, and cowboy hats. We walked on stage carrying guitars, and sang our own lyrics to a country western tune. None of us knew how to play a guitar but we strummed along anyway. We weren't afraid of making fools of ourselves; we were just having fun. It was the one day we could drop our strict professional demeanor in front of the staff.

There were other groups that participated in the talent show. When the "California Raisins" commercials were popular, one department dressed as raisins. They sang and danced around the stage while we all sang along. Even the children entered the talent show by singing, dancing, or acrobatics. The show was the highlight of the picnic.

The hospital paid for the food, and there was a lot of it. While the adults played softball or badminton, or tossed horseshoes, the children ran around chasing each other with water balloons. There were other activities for the kids, including tossing eggs. That could get a little messy. My youngest son's strongest memory of PT was from one of these picnics. With her hair exquisitely styled, she called out to the kids throwing water balloons. "Don't get my hair wet!" There was no degree of joking in her admonition. The other staff members and I laughed. We all knew how PT was about her hair.

The annual picnic was a fun time to get together with employees from all shifts and relax. Later when the hospital joined a larger health care network, there was a several-year hiatus in the picnics. About five years before I retired, however, we did have another one. The hospital provided the food and drinks and the employees brought desserts. A couple of different games were added—bean bag toss and bingo. It was a nice affair, but smaller and quieter than our old ones. Everyone more or less stayed in their own groups. To me, it didn't have the same group identity atmosphere of the old picnics. Times were changing for the hospital.

# CHAPTER 16

## *Back to Class*

The smell of formaldehyde filled the room. My lab partner and I looked at the scrawny creature on the table before us. I remembered thinking that they must have found this one in an alley. Fortunately, my lab partner was a hunter and didn't mind doing that first task that I dreaded, the skinning. It was 1984, and who would imagine that after more than two decades of nursing, I would again find myself with a scalpel in my hand reluctantly preparing to dissect a cat. I cringed inside. This procedure had been one of my least favorite aspects of nursing school. Ugh! So, how did I get here?

It all began a few years prior, at a nurse managers' meeting at the hospital. The Director of Nursing matter-of-factly told the nurse managers, nine or ten of us, that we all needed to obtain a Bachelor of Science in Nursing, the BSN degree. The hospital would reimburse some of the costs. All of the nurse managers at the meeting had, like me, started their careers through a three-year nursing program, a full 36 months of classes and clinicals at a hospital. Some nurse managers felt obtaining a BSN was unnecessary. They had been successfully practicing in the field for many years, and didn't feel that their management style would be changed to a degree meriting the time and money poured into a BSN degree. I knew that as a full-time night shift employee and mother of five children—spread out in ages from a kindergartener to a high school senior—the effort could prove exhausting. However, this new requirement secretly stirred my old desire to obtain a university degree. I would begin the program at Pennsylvania State University.

When I told my parents that I would be starting my bachelor's program, they were happy for me. They knew it was something I had always dreamed of. My father especially was proud; his daughter, already a practicing nurse, was going to earn a university degree. When I told my husband and children that I would be starting my BSN degree, I got a different reaction—confusion. They wanted to know why I was pursuing a degree in a field I was already qualified for and practicing in full-time. Many of the university instructors had the same reaction when they discovered seasoned nurses in the student seats.

My first day in "Nursing 101," I chatted with my fellow students before class, and found out that other hospitals were also requesting their experienced nurses without BSNs to enroll in a program. The Nursing 101 instructor did not know what to do with these students. Everything she would teach us we already knew. She went back to the university administration and obtained permission for us to complete our class by participating in a wellness fair at a shopping mall. We took vital signs, tested blood, educated people, and wrote a paper documenting our work. We all felt that holding the wellness fair was a good decision on the instructor's part. In lieu of reading about processes we already knew *very well*, we assisted the local community in its health needs. Another class in which the instructor revised the curriculum was Geriatrics. At a senior residential home, the students instructed a class for caregivers. Our focus was informing caregivers of available resources and of how to ensure that in caring for others, they also took care of themselves.

Most the classes, however, were straight book work. Many of the nurses were upset to have to take basic nursing classes again. A few nurses received some credit from their three-year program. This was given only if the three-year nursing program was associated with a university. However, for the rest of us, we received no credit, *zero*, for our three-year diploma and many years of practice. I was happy to be on my way to a bachelor's degree; nonetheless, I felt it was a slap in the face that the university started me on a blank slate. It was a disrespect to my in-depth and hands-on South Side nursing education and years of work experience. I felt it wasn't fair then, and looking back today, I know it was not fair.

Given my job and family commitments, I took classes when I could. This was the 1980s, well prior to online classes. The other nurses and I had chosen Penn State, because we were informed that we could complete all classes in nearby Washington, Pennsylvania. However, after we all had taken a few classes, the university informed us that the program would no longer be available in Washington. We had to choose another location. I decided to take classes at the Fayette campus. This resulted in me driving two hours round trip two or three times a week to take classes. Scheduling required classes in a time frame I could attend was not always easy. It took me ten years to earn my BSN.

When I started the BSN program, I was in my early 40s, and I initially felt out of place being in class with 19- and 20-year-olds. After a few classes, however, I got used to it. I took the required nursing classes such as Anatomy, Chemistry, Psychology, Obstetrics, Pediatrics. Most of my classes were a repeat of what I had learned in nursing school, but with updated material and much less clinical time. In fact, when we did clinical time at a hospital, we were primarily just observing.

In my three-year nursing school, all classes and clinics pertained to nursing. Now, to earn my bachelor's degree, I had to study other fields. I was eagerly curious to see what classes I could take to fulfill my electives. One of my favorite electives was Art History. I had had little exposure to this field. I admired the artwork in the required course book, and still have my book to this day. When it came time to take a physical education class, however, I had some trepidation. I pictured myself playing a sport with students half my age. And while I considered myself to be in decent shape—spending most my working hours on my feet—I had very little experience in organized sports. I was uncertain of what sport I could passably participate in with the other students. Then I saw it on the course list—golf. A purely non-contact activity, and I comforted myself with the thought that I was a pretty good putt-putt golfer. Alas, this sport was harder than I anticipated. Our "Final Exam" was playing nine holes. Let's just say that I was more than a bit over par, but I got my physical education credit checked off.

My least favorite class was Statistics. I only enrolled because I was informed that should I go on to a master's degree program, this class was a prerequisite. I found the subject dry and tedious. And I was fortunate to be in the class with a well-reputed professor. I'm not sure how I would have done in another professor's class. The material simply did not find a welcoming place in my brain. I had to put extra effort into this class. Notwithstanding, I managed a decent grade. I don't recall the exact grade, but I never earned less than a B in any of my BSN courses.

During this ten-year period, my children often saw me retreat to the downstairs den after dinner to study. Years later, one of my daughters asked me to what degree my BSN had improved my nursing techniques. I paused a long while before responding. I wanted to say how the time-consuming effort had transformed my nursing practice. I wanted to speak of the new skills I had obtained. Ultimately, however, I had to be honest. "Truthfully, I don't think it did." I added that, nevertheless, I believed the degree program had improved me as a person, broadening my general knowledge. And, ultimately, I was glad to have my degree.

Having experienced both programs—a three-year nursing school and a BSN program—I could see the pros and cons of each. To me the greatest difference lies in the clinical preparedness of new nurses. As a student, when I worked the evening or night shift at South Side Hospital,

I might have 20 to 25 patients. The BSN students did not experience this. When I started as a registered nurse in 1962, I jumped straight into a routine of a full patient load. I felt prepared; I had handled as much as a student. Also, each of my South Side academic classes had been accompanied by comprehensive hands-on application of the course material.

As a nursing supervisor, it seemed to me that the BSN students were geared toward administrative positions, rather than hands-on patient care. It would take a new nurse several months to become acclimated to full nursing responsibilities. At my hospital, we put them on an orientation program with an experienced nurse for several months. One night, one of my nurses who was orienting a recent BSN graduate came to me upset. She said that she could only give the new nurse one patient. "That is all she can handle at this time, and we are *so* busy." Similar issues arose with the nurses who had recently graduated from a two-year school of nursing that had focused more on classroom education and not the clinical experience. Occasionally, these new nurses would come to me overwhelmed by their duties. Sometimes they were at the end of their orientation, the point we expected them to take on a regular assignment. I would inform these nurses that they needed to learn how to better manage their time, but that I would talk to the unit manager and see if she would extend the period of orientation. Usually, the manager agreed to this, but with the understanding that if the nurse could not handle a regular assignment by the end of the extended orientation, she would not be retained.

While new graduates from the BSN programs may have lacked the clinical finesse to efficiently insert a catheter or an NG tube, my greater disappointment was their inexperience at patient assessment. With experience, a good nurse can walk into a room and, with a visual assessment, nearly immediately know the patient's pain level, changes in physical condition, whether they need oxygen or other treatment, or whether a doctor should be called. This skill, this intuition, only comes with hands-on caring for patients. These new hires did, of course, become excellent nurses, but they first needed the on-floor time that was lacking from their BSN programs.

I remember my BSN graduation day clearly. It was May 1990. The ceremony was at the branch campus of Penn State, where I had taken most of my classes. I was seated front row. In attendance were several of my family members—children, in-laws, my mother. My father was now deceased. However, I felt that he, who was always so proud of me and my nursing career, was there in spirit. My name was called. As I walked across the stage, I could feel the weight of ten-years of educational commitment lifted from me. This chapter was successfully finished. Of the small group of nurse managers from my hospital that started the BSN program years prior, I was the only one to finish. I graduated with honors.

~ ~ ~

Fast-forward to September 1992. My friend and I were walking from the parking lot to the building where we would attend our first class in a master's program. Seeing the class building a short distance away brought back the weighty feeling of having my non-work hours filled with driving, classes, writing papers, studying. "What am I doing here? Why am I doing this to myself." Nonetheless, the master's program had a professional draw for me. In fact, during the majority of my BSN program, I knew I would go on to a master's degree. I wanted to expand my knowledge to advance in my career. As I mentioned, that is the only reason I slogged through that Statistics course. And by 1992, I should have been recharged; I had taken two glorious gap years from my BSN graduation to the start my master's program. I had enjoyed reading books that were not required text books. I took the time off from formal studies so that I could attend my youngest child's high school soccer games and other extracurricular events. He had graduated May 1992. So, no excuses now.

I chose to pursue a master's degree not in Nursing but in Health Services Administration. I felt this would give me a broader area of study, and potentially position me for a job in health administration—*a day job*. After working a quarter century on night shift, a day job seemed like a dream. I could imagine myself arriving at work in the morning and leaving in the late afternoon, like most employees.

I selected the University of St. Francis, after speaking with a graduate from the program. The campus was a 45-minute drive away. I was fortunate to have a fellow nurse from Canonsburg Hospital start and finish the degree program with me. Joyce was an Intensive Care nurse. When I told her that I was going to enroll in a master's program, she said she wanted to attain her master's also. We were both excited about the program, as well as attending together. We submitted our applications. There was one major frustration waiting for me. I was missing a prerequisite. The university informed me that I needed an Accounting class. I asked about my Statistics course. Apparently, it was not Statistics that I needed after all. Therefore, the summer before I started my masters, I took the required Accounting class at a junior college.

Joyce and I took turns driving to campus. On regular class days, we would chat mainly about our personal lives and daily events. On exam days, we quizzed each other during the commute. I knew I was fortunate to have such a good companion to car pool with. We remain good friends to this day.

The educational atmosphere of the master's program was vastly different to me than my BSN program. The students were seasoned professionals from a broad spectrum of the healthcare field. They were more mature, more knowledge-hungry. The professors, with one unnamed exception, recognized the students as professionals and respected our opinions. We had meaningful exchanges of ideas in the classes. In a few of the classes, the professors would use the debate technique—assigning students a topic and position to research and defend. Watching the debates was like going to a live performance. The exchange of ideas made me want to do broader research, beyond the issues I saw at a small community hospital. In fact, after graduation, I began to miss this intellectual stimulation.

The camaraderie was high. After each final, many students met at T.G.I. Fridays to celebrate one more class accomplished. The students also began meeting before class at a food court in a nearby mall. We got to know each other well, as we counted down the classes. Joyce and I would drive to campus early, not just to avoid traffic but to eat with the other students before class. I still laugh about a birthday present she gave me before class. When we arrived, Joyce said, "You're coming with me." We walked through the mall, and I voiced objection when we stopped in front of Piercing Pagoda. I was 54 and had never pierced my ears. Instead I wore the uncomfortable clip-ons. Joyce said, "You're getting your ears pierced. I'm paying." She had previously asked me about my clip-ons, and I told her that maybe one day I would get piercings. With trepidation, I consented. About an hour later, I went to class with my starter studs.

I finished the program in three years. Graduation was held at the main campus in Joliet, Illinois—450 miles away. Students could elect to attend in person or have the diploma mailed to them. I did not have to think twice about these options. I worked hard for this degree and was proud of my 3.8 grade point average. I booked a flight to Chicago. My oldest daughter came with me. At the Chicago airport, we rented a car and drove to the campus. That evening there was a dinner for the master's candidates. I was graduating with honors, and received a beautiful plaque commemorating my achievement.

The morning of graduation, there was another meal for the graduating master's class. This was a nice touch. After breakfast, the friends and family members walked to the outdoor pavilion where the ceremony would be held, while the graduates donned caps and gowns. We then walked, on the pleasant sunny day, down a long street to the graduation site. It was a beautiful feeling being decked in my graduation attire, strolling in a stream of like-clad achievers, with supporting friends and family members awaiting our arrival. At the ceremony, my name was called and I walked on stage to receive my diploma and have the hood placed on me. The master's degree was well worth the time, effort, and energy I put in it. I did not have to travel 450 miles to know that. But walking on stage with the other graduates felt like a dream.

# CHAPTER 17

## *The Deposition*

Opposing counsel was interrogating one of my staff nurses. "Are you taking classes toward your BSN?" she grilled. "No," replied my staff nurse. The quick soft sound of the stenographer's typing underscored the significance of the exchange. I had been in nursing for more than twenty years, and it was my first deposition. The exchange continued. "And why not?" The nurse replied, "I am not seeking a job in administration." This made perfect sense to me. At that time, nurses who had been trained in a three-year nursing school, as I had, did not additionally work towards a BSN degree unless they were in an administrative position. However, the opposing counsel felt this was grounds to discredit the nurse. "Are you sure you know how to take care of patients with just a three-year nursing degree?" How dare she! I wanted to rise up out of my chair and defend my staff nurse.

Three nurses and I, as supervisor, were called to testify in depositions. These were held in a conference room in our hospital. The attorneys and stenographer sat at a table, while the other nurses and I sat in chairs to the rear of the table. We were individually called to the table to testify. I was surprised to find that we were all present in one room and could hear each other responses. I'm not a lawyer, but this just didn't seem right to me . . . But I'm glad I could hear the nurses' answers. I knew they had not done anything wrong, and I was glad to see them stand up for themselves.

When it was my turn to be deposed, the attorney asked me about my educational background. As I was enrolled in a BSN program at the time, she didn't further pursue the issue with me, as she had done with my staff. In the deposition, I explained my observations and actions that night.

The information provided in the depositions showed that the nurses had done their job. Nonetheless, I left the depositions with indignation. To me it was ignorant and unprofessional for the plaintiff's attorney to demean the three nurses for obtaining their professional education and training in a three-year nursing school. These all were excellent nurses, and I wish I had been given the opportunity to rebut the insinuation that they needed a BSN to adequately care for patients.

I was on the second floor on the night in question. The nurses were making first rounds. An elderly woman had surgery that day, and I went into the room to see how she was doing. The nurse was present and was explaining to the patient that she was not to get up by herself. The nurse showed her how to put the call light on if she needed anything or had to use the bathroom. A couple hours later on my next round, I was at the nurses' station when we heard a crash. Running into the room, we found the patient lying on the floor. She didn't appear injured, but I had the ER doctor check her. He gave her an all clear. The patient explained that she felt that she could go to the bathroom by herself; she did not want to bother anyone. The family filed a lawsuit, claiming we were negligent.

The case was eventually dropped; there was neither negligence nor an injury. I will never forget, however, how the plaintiff's attorney put the nurses down for completing their professional education at a three-year nursing school and not further pursuing a BSN. I was angry that these excellent nurses were criticized with this ignorant position.

While that was my first deposition, it was not my last. Yet, for a medical professional, I seemed to have escaped the average number of involvements in lawsuits. I only had one other deposition in my career. In the last third of my career, it certainly seemed to me that medical professionals, particularly the doctors, were more frequently subjected to lawsuits. Sometimes patients used the threat of a lawsuit in attempt to get the doctor to order a specific treatment. As a supervisor, I heard it many times, especially from medication-seekers in the ER. The threat of a lawsuit would be the last I-still-have-power remark as they stomped out of the building.

The second case involved an elderly woman on the telemetry unit who went into cardiac arrest. Code Blue was called and we started CPR. I was the scribe. This means that I documented on the code sheet every-thing that happened. This is required for all codes. The scribe also writes the time for each procedure and medication. The clock on the wall behind the patient's bed, visible to all, is used as the official time. This way, all staff are working from the same clock. If the doctor asks when a medica-tion was last given, the scribe will reference the code sheet and provide the time; comparison with the clock on the wall provides an accurate measure of time for everyone. We worked for several minutes but could not revive the patient. Two years later the family sued, citing negligence.

I was informed of the lawsuit at a managers' meeting. From the patient's name, I could not recall the specific incident. I obtained the medical records to refresh my memory, spoke with the hospital attor-neys, and prepared for the deposition. Everyone working the code was deposed—the doctor, the respiratory therapist, the three staff nurses, and me. This time, we all had separate scheduled times for the individ-ual depositions and did not witness each other's testimony.

When I was deposed, I answered all questions regarding the pro-cedure we had performed. Through her questions, the plaintiff's attor-ney reached far to try to insinuate a cover up. She asked me why the times I wrote down were different than the ones on the cardiac strips printed from the machine. I explained that since clocks, watches, and monitors can all be a minute or two different, we always use the wall clock in the patient's room during a code. That way everyone is following the same time for medications and procedures. The attorney didn't like my answer and said, "All clocks should be the same time. You need to fix those." Obviously, she never worked in a hospital.

A few weeks after the deposition, I received a letter from the hospital attorney saying we were going to court, and I would be notified of the day and time. I would have to make arrangements to be off work the night before. In all my years of nursing, I had not testified in court, and I was not looking forward to it. A couple weeks later, I received the follow-up letter. Resigned to the fact that I had to testify, I opened the letter to find out the date. The letter informed me, however, that the case had settled out of court. I was thoroughly relieved.

I always told my staff to chart everything. If it's not charted, no matter what you say, the perception will be that you hadn't done it.

# CHAPTER 18

## *Changing Times*

The patient was in cardiac arrest. The respiratory therapist was bagging the lungs, an ER nurse and a paramedic were taking turns giving the chest compressions, and I was administering the medications, all pursuant to the doctor's orders. The patient did not respond. As we continued working, we listened for the doctor's next order or decision to call it. What I heard from him was not what I was expecting or had heard before in my close to 25 years of nursing. "Can anybody think of anything else we could try?"

We all replied in the negative. He then said, "I'm going to call it. Is it okay with everybody?" Everyone agreed. There was nothing more we could do for the patient. I was left with a satisfied feeling from this experience. It was very unusual for a doctor to seek opinions from the nursing staff. Yet, the nurses, especially the more experienced nurses, certainly had knowledge and opinions regarding the care of patients. We were not doctors, yet our assessments could provide additional insight that a doctor could use in care decisions. When I first started nursing, the doctors did not ask professional opinions of the nurses. As a student nurse at South Side, I basically learned that the doctor was a god, and the nurses were subordinate. Even if we had an opinion on a potential course of care, we would not dare offer it to a doctor. Now, in the 1980s, my opinion was asked for. I truly felt like part of a patient-care *team*. The doctor was lead, but I was a knowledgeable and skilled team member.

It was during this time of increasing teamwork, that there was a decrease in the rigid gender stereotypes. Before we had moved to the new hospital in 1983, I had only worked with one female doctor and zero male nurses. Now in the new ER, I worked with both a female doctor and a male nurse. I was happy to see women becoming medical doctors and welcomed men to the nursing field. However, the latter was somewhat odd to me at first. When I began nursing school in 1958, there were no males admitted to our program, and in all my training I never saw one male nurse. At the 1961 nursing board examination, with candidates from across Pennsylvania, I did not see a male candidate. In my time in California, I did not work with any male nurses. Given the culture in which I began my nursing career, the image of a nurse to me was always female. Having spent three years in an all-female dormitory for nursing school only solidified that image. It was not that I felt males would be lesser qualified to perform nursing duties, it was just that it didn't fit the mold I was groomed in. For medical care by non-physicians, that meant women were nurses, men could be paramedics. Professionally, I did not expect more or less from the male nurses; I demanded the same standards from all my staff. Over my career, I saw the borders for the medical fields dissolve for both genders. Women became accepted as physicians, and men as nurses. This allows professionals to serve in the area they feel most called to and are best gifted to perform.

During the same time period, many nurses began pursuing careers in more advanced nursing fields, specialties that were not available when I graduated from nursing school. This included, for example, nurse practitioners and nurse anesthetists. Had I been younger, I could have seen myself pursuing a nurse practitioner license. When I was starting my career, there were many times that in my mind I formulated a treatment plan for a patient, but I would not dare suggest it to a doctor. Now, years later, enjoying my supervisor duties and burdened with classes for a BSN, I felt it was too late in my career to change vectors. However, I was glad to see these opportunities for nurses.

It was also during the 1980s that doctors began requesting that nurses call them by their first names. At our hospital, it was more prevalent in the ER, where the doctors and nurses worked closely together each night. Given the etiquette rules ingrained in me from nursing school, and 25 years of formally addressing doctors, this was a difficult change for me. Therefore, I did not always comply with the request, and when I did, I was not always fully comfortable with it. Over the years, it became easier for me to call a doctor by his or her first name, but there was still that little voice in me telling me I was breaking a rule.

While the old etiquette protocols were disappearing, the new hospital did institute a few new policies. We now had written standards on personal appearance for nurses and nursing assistants. Early in my nursing career at Canonsburg, there was not a written appearance policy, nor, in my opinion, a need for it then. We were all "old school" in our appearance. We had been drilled in nursing school in the proper way to present ourselves—from impeccable uniforms, polished shoes, short or pinned-up hair, minimal jewelry and no visible necklaces. And there had been no need to address facial piercings or visible tattoos. Now in the 1980s, the younger staff were more relaxed in their professional appearance. The new written rules addressed not only cleanliness of uniform, but hair length, permissible jewelry, body piercings, visible tattoos, nail polish color. Even type of nail polish was addressed. Gel nail polish was not permitted as it was thought to be more susceptible to bacteria collecting. One of my responsibilities in the non-clinical category was ensuring the staff complied with the dress code. If I did not catch a transgression, the day-shift unit manager would ask me why I had not addressed the issue with the employee. Primarily what I ended up discussing with employees was jewelry that a disruptive patient could grab and hair that needed to be pinned up. Discussions regarding visible tattoos came later in my career.

A bigger change was the nursing uniform. First, we went from all white to the option of navy blue, for either the top or the pants or both. In the early 1980's, I began wearing navy blue pants with my traditional white top, nurses cap, and lab jacket. I found that the blue pants looked cleaner, especially on nights I had to do blood transfusions. On those nights, I often got blood on my pants. When I wore white pants, this was more of a problem. I would put peroxide on the pants I was wearing and try to scrub away the stain. Sometimes, I could not remove the stain that evening. So, I preferred the blue pants.

A few years later, I saw an even more significant change in the nurse's uniform. Nurses began wearing scrubs, not only in the ER. At first, the scrubs were white or navy blue, like the more traditional pants and tops. Then each unit selected a color to designate the staff of their unit. Soon, everyone began wearing scrubs, even the housekeeping staff. However, there were a few holdouts. One of our ER nurses was a former Army nurse who was old school, very formal. No one called her by her first name, simply her last name with no title. That is what she preferred. She was a tiny woman, but her presence was always known. She was a no-nonsense person who smoked like a fiend. She was the last to convert to the scrubs. With the rest of the ER nurses in the same color scrubs, she finally gave in. But to her, it wasn't a proper nurse's uniform.

Before scrubs became common wear, there was what I considered a much sadder change to the uniform. In the early 80's, caps were quickly disappearing. The new nurses did not wear the traditional cap, and almost all of the older nurses had stopped wearing theirs by the mid-1980s. At one point, it was only PT and me left wearing our nurses' caps. I told her, "We're the last two wearing caps." She replied, "I will never give mine up." At that time, I had the same sentiment. I had gone with the flow of the previous uniform changes, but this was the hardest part for me. My cap completed my professional uniform. When nurses stopped wearing the cap, I was asked by patients and family members about it. They were frustrated that they could not tell who was a nurse as opposed to aides and other staff. With only PT and me left, I was the next-to-last to dispense of the cap. It was more because of sabotage than a purposeful decision by me to abandon the tradition.

I always left my cap in the bottom left-hand drawer of my desk in a plastic bag. I did this for years, in the same location of the desk. One night, I entered the supervisor's office to receive my report from PT. I opened the drawer to get my cap, and found a heavy book lying on top of my cap. I had recently washed, starched, ironed and folded my cap. The folding was a complicated matter in which I placed a can on each side of the cap so when the starch dried, the folds would stay in place. Now, my perfect cap was flattened. I demanded, "Who did this? Who put this book here?" PT, still in cap, looked sadly at the smashed cap, shook her head, and said, "I didn't do it." So, feeling not completely dressed, I went without my cap that night. People asked "Where's your cap?" I told them indignantly that someone had squashed it with a book. Afterwards, I didn't have the heart to prepare another. Yet, for a long time, I did not feel properly dressed for my profession without my cap. Even after I stopped wearing mine, PT continued. She was the last nurse at Canonsburg Hospital that I saw carry the cherished tradition.

# CHAPTER 19

## *The Strike*

Screaming angrily, she ran along the side of my car as I slowly drove down the hospital road to the employee parking lot. Then I saw her spit on the driver's door. It was 1991 and the strike had begun—a strike that would shock the staff with its hostility.

In the weeks prior, the administrators and nurse managers were aware that the contract with much of the support staff—nurses' aides, housekeeping, maintenance, and kitchen workers—was ending. Renegotiations with the union were not successful, and we were informed that these workers would strike. They had gone on strike in years past, and we made preparations as we felt necessary. We prepared for a two-week strike, expecting that, as in years past, the two sides would reach an agreement. We prepared a work schedule that included more nurses per shift; additional supplies were stocked; the kitchen manager ordered more food and managers were scheduled to help with the preparation. As with past strikes, we expected the support staff to peacefully picket at the ends of the road for the hospital entrances until a contract could be negotiated.

From day one, however, a hatefulness, a maliciousness, came to the forefront. The managers and nurses became the target for this hatefulness. I want to believe that by themselves, the support staff would have protested civilly to their ends, and the contract would have been successfully renegotiated in a short time, with hospital staff returning to a professional and collegial work environment. None of that happened, however. A call went out to other union members to come and support the strike at the hospital. My brother-in-law in a neighboring town informed me that his teachers' union was called. As the hospital strike progressed, it seemed to me that it became for many a license to behave maliciously. A crowd mentality prevailed over wise and diplomatic strategies. The strike lasted 149 days. The focus on the contract issues seemed lost in the malice. And, in my opinion, what the strikers ultimately gained was certainly no greater than would have been achieved in a shorter time if they had demonstrated their position peacefully.

In this heated environment, I saw the mentality of aides I worked with completely change. Obscenities were shouted at managers and nurses as they came and went from the hospital. One pregnant nurse manager had her car violently rocked back and forth as she attempted to drive down the entrance way. Another nurse had a wood strip with nails placed behind her tire when it was in the employee parking lot. The strikers blocked both entrances to the hospital, and lined the roads to parking lots. They stopped the vehicles of individuals taking family members to the ER and told them to go to another hospital. They even attempted to stop ambulances. One of the drivers told me he refused to turn away with his patient and slowly drove through the crowd.

One of my sons had a chronic disease that required him to have regular blood analysis. This was not an option. I drove him to the hospital one afternoon for the blood work. As I drove down the entrance road, strikers ran along both sides of my car screaming and hitting the car. My son was feeling sick, and I was very upset that he had to experience this hatefulness on his way to receive medical care.

I kept the nasty details of the strike from my mother. She was 81, living by herself, and showing her age. I visited and assisted her daily. If she asked me about something regarding the strike that she saw on the news, I downplayed it. I did not want to worry her.

The hospital obtained a court order limiting the strikers to one entrance, prohibiting them from stopping vehicles coming or going, and prohibiting them from entering the hospital grounds. Before we obtained the court order, one of the administrators videotaped the strikers from a rooftop vantage point. It was years later that I saw the video. When that subsequent contract was due to expire, the administrator who made the videotape played a short clip at one of the management meetings. He wanted us to know what extreme behavior the staff was capable of. We watched strikers lying down on the road to block cars coming to the hospital, others running alongside the cars, screaming and hitting the vehicles.

One night I was getting the shift report from PT, and she told me she had seen the strikers crawling in the grass towards the hospital. They crawled army-style, as if they were preparing to ambush an enemy. "They were crawling up the hill! I don't know what they were going to do, but they were crawling up the hill like soldiers!" She said she called security, and security contacted the police, who made the people return to the picket area. It was a scary time; no one knew what these individuals were capable of. We had already seen the expressions of hate.

The strikers took their hate off-campus. We knew that the strikers had the home addresses of management. Apparently, they had the supervisors' addresses also. One evening as I was sitting in my living room, I heard a loud bang against the house. I found a large rock lying below my picture window. It had hit the front of my house, likely intended for the window. A member of the board of directors lived a few houses down from me. The strikers blocked the street in front his house. I could hear the chanting from my house. This action was repeated at different times on other days. I was informed that this was done to all the board members.

A group of strikers also chanted outside one of the board member's place of business.

Even if they wanted to, it became dangerous for workers to come back during the strike. This was a dilemma for some of our workers who were the sole income earners of their families. After a few weeks, a couple of aides did return to work, but did so clandestinely, hiding in cars of nurses as they came and went to the hospital. After the strike, other support staff told me that they had wanted to come to work, but were afraid to do so, as they feared that they or their family would be retaliated against. The fear was legitimate. One of the workers who did cross the line found all the windows in his car broken. Worse occurred to a painting contractor who came to finish his job during the strike. He was not a support staff member, yet, he found his dog shot dead that day. When I heard this, I could not believe how low people of my community had sunken. My husband came from Pittsburgh steel worker roots, and I had certainly supported the right for unions to advocate for better pay and benefits, and the right of workers to strike. However, the means used here—the ugly harassment and threat of violence against individuals—put this union on par with thugs in my mind. At that point, I honestly did not care if any of the strikers came back to work.

During the strike, the patient census dropped to about half the normal number. However, even without the support staff, patients were well-cared for. We had one or two extra nurses on each unit. Given the decreased patient load and additional nurses, the care, in my opinion, was excellent. Patients received more personal care time from the nurses than under normal circumstances. In fact, nurses occasionally found themselves with extra time. One night, I saw a nurse entering the nurses' lounge with a wash pan filled with soapy water. I asked her what she was doing. She said she was cleaning the walls. Just a few minutes later she came out to refresh the soap and water in the wash pan. When she saw me, she said, "Come and look." I entered the lounge with her. She had cleaned about half the wall. One half was white, the other half was grey.

The lounge had served as the smoking room for nurses on their breaks. We never realized that over time the cigarette smoke had gradually changed the color of the walls. She picked up a sponge and began scrubbing diligently. "This is disgusting!"

Ultimately, the strike was resolved, with the assistance of a mediator, and the support staff returned to work. It appeared to me that, surprisingly, they expected the normal workplace harmony. It was understandably not there. Not even close. A lot of friendships were lost. I was cordial to all the support staff, even those that had engaged in vile behavior. To be completely honest, this was done out of necessity for professionalism in the workplace, not out of sincerity. It took a few years for the community to feel comfortable coming back to our hospital; the hospital census remained low in the years immediately following the strike.

# CHAPTER 20

# *IV Team*

It was 1991. The Director of Nursing (DON) had requested that I come to her office for a mid-afternoon meeting. No topic was given. I scanned my memory for anything amiss in my recent work but could not guess the issue. I finished the night shift, took a short nap, and came back for the meeting. When I arrived at her office, she got straight to the matter. I was offered the responsibilities of the Director of the IV Team, in additional to my regular duties. At the time, the IV team was led by a Director of another unit. She no longer wanted the extra duties. This should have been my first clue; this additional job came with many responsibilities but no salary increase. Nonetheless, I was persuaded to accept the position. The DON said it would be good for me to learn how to do the budget, hiring, and the general operation of a small department. This alone did not convince me to accept the position. The big pull for me was her promise to give me the next available position of a unit director. While the supervisor is in charge of the entire hospital for a specific shift, a director is in charge of a specific nursing unit—such as ICU, ambulatory care, or a med-surg unit—for all operations 24/7. *A day shift job!* After more than two decades of working night shift, the thought of working daylight hours was intoxicating. I could not say no to a potential path to removing the light-blocking material from my bedroom windows, going to bed at the same time as the rest of my family, and waking up with the early morning sun.

I started my duties that week. The IV team had two full-time nurses, two part-time nurses, and two nurses who worked PRN (as needed). Their duties were to start all IVs, change the dressings on IVs and central lines, and perform blood transfusions. There were a few exceptions. One was ER; the ER RNs would continue to perform IVs. Another exception was ICU, although the IV team often assisted when needed. The final exception was the night shift. I had to assume these responsibilities. This was not exactly a supervisor's duties, but it certainly kept my IV skills optimal. Although ICU did their own IVs, I was seen as a resource to perform "difficult sticks." When an ICU nurse could not find a decent vein, I would be paged.

There is some art to inserting an IV, and there were a number of patients who presented challenges. On patients with sleeve tattoos, for example, it is quite difficult to view the veins. After applying a tourniquet, when a vein was not visible, I would feel for it. With my fingertips, I would push lightly on the arm where I knew a vein should be, and most often could find it by feel. For obese patients, the challenge was locating the correct depth for the vein. And some patients simply do not have adequate veins for IVs. For one patient, I had to insert the IV on the top of the foot, so she could receive her medication.

As Director of the IV team, I held monthly staff meetings in the afternoon. I briefed the team on policy updates and we reviewed any current issues or problems they wanted to discuss. Additionally, I now attended the monthly directors' meetings, held during day shift hours, of course. I was given an annual budget to manage. This included salaries, equipment, educational supplies and conferences. I maintained the "policy and procedure" books with the help of the IV team. These were subject to periodic inspections by the state and Joint Commission on

Accreditation of Healthcare Organizations. I primarily did the paperwork at home, outside my shift hours. I also reviewed and approved the team's work schedule. Once, a 3-to-11 IV nurse called off, and a replacement could not be found. Therefore, I worked her 3-to-11 shift, then covered my night shift. These were all additional duties within my regular salary.

The League of Intravenous Therapy held a two-day seminar at Allegheny General Hospital (AGH) in Pittsburgh every year. For several years, I was able to budget for my team to attend one of the two days, and I was able to attend both days. We met with IV nurses from many hospitals and exchanged ideas and learned new procedures. It was always very informative, and I looked forward to the seminar. This is where I first heard of the PICC line. The PICC line—peripherally inserted central catheter—is a long slim catheter inserted into the upper arm and advanced to a large vein in the chest just above the heart. We used it for long-term antibiotics, medications, blood draws, and intravenously administered nutrition. The PICC line can stay in the patient for several weeks or months, making multiple IV insertions unnecessary. In contrast, we generally changed the standard IV every 72 hours. Several months after the seminar, the IV team and I were all trained at AGH to insert and care for PICC lines.

Our training consisted of shadowing an AGH IV nurse, specifically the nurse assigned PICC lines, for an entire shift. During that time, we had to observe her insert a PICC line, and then, under her observation, insert three successfully. After each insertion, radiology checked the placement. In addition to inserting the new PICC lines, we would follow the IV nurse on her rounds, checking PICC lines. She would carefully measure the section of the line outside the body to ensure the line had not moved; she would change dressings as needed and check the condition of the insertion site. Each member of my IV team went for this training on a different day. Before I went for my training, one of the nurses who had just completed the shift at AGH informed me that she would need to do another training day there. The issue was not her skill, but that she only had two PICC lines to insert that day. No other patients had needed the procedure. I hoped this would not happen to me. On the day I went, I did a 7 a.m. to 3 p.m. shift. The first need for the procedure came early in the shift, and I observed the IV nurse insert a PICC line. Three more procedures were necessary for me to complete the training. Before lunch, I had successfully performed two. I needed one more procedure. I checked the clock every 15 minutes or so. At one point, there were about 90 minutes remaining in the shift, and I started to become concerned I would have to return another day. The procedure took approximately half an hour. We had to: examine the patient's arm; measure the distance of the area where the insertion would be threaded (elbow to shoulder and across the chest to the area over the heart); don sterile gown, mask and gloves; open a sterile tray; sterilize the patient's skin at the insertion site, and begin the insertion procedure which required slow threading of the line. Then when we were finished, we had to bring the patient to radiology to have the position of the PICC line checked via X-ray. I wondered if I would get one more procedure in. Then around two o'clock, the IV nurse was paged. I listened closely to the information relayed. Another patient needed a PICC line. This would be my third procedure. I successfully finished three procedures, and was now qualified to perform these at Canonsburg Hospital.

Soon after my team had been qualified to insert PICC lines, the decision was made to move these duties to the ambulatory care nurses. I do not know the rationale for this change. However, eventually, the responsibility was given to radiology. Now this made sense to me. Since the patient had to be moved to radiology to have the PICC line checked, it made sense to have the procedure performed by that unit.

A few years after learning the PICC line, my team and I were introduced to another new technology—ports. Ports allowed repeated access to a patient's main vein without having to pierce the skin with a regular IV needle. The port was inserted by a surgeon or radiologist. It is a small drum made of plastic or metal with a rubber like seal across the top. A thin tube goes from the drum into the vein. When needed for blood draws or medications, it is accessed with a special needle. Ports can stay in a patient for several years. The first time I was called to access a port was on a patient in the ER. The technology was so new, I had never seen a port, let alone accessed one. Nonetheless, as the IV team Director, I kept up with medical literature and ensured we had procedures and equipment in place to be prepared for this technology. While the ER RNs normally started their own IVs, when the first patient with a port presented, the RN paged me. I was told, "We have a patient with a port. We need it accessed." I didn't go straight to the ER, but to the IV office, where I pulled out the procedure that I had placed in the policies/procedures book. I read it carefully. Then I read it again. I gathered the needed equipment for the procedure, took a deep breath, and headed down to the ER. I introduced myself to the patient, placed the equipment on the table, and explained that I was going to access her port. I tried to appear confident. I did not want the patient to suspect that this would actually be my first time performing the procedure. I swabbed around the port area, wiped the top of the port, opened a sterile needle, applied the syringe filled with saline. I inserted the needle in the port, and pulled the plunger of the syringe to ensure that blood flow in the vein was properly accessed. Success. There was a separate procedure for removing the syringe when the patient would be discharged; I went back to the office and read it.

While my first port access went smoothly, I soon found they were not all this easy. Depending on how the port's tube was positioned, it could be difficult to get blood flow back. This could be remedied sometimes by having the patient raise his or her arm, which readjusted the tube. This fix was not in the procedure manual. I learned it from a patient. After I made an unsuccessful attempt at access, the patient told me, "Sometimes this helps," and then raised his arm up over his head. It worked.

As the only "IV team" person working night shift, I was soon performing all port accesses. At first, I'd see only one or two per month. As ports became more prevalent, I would do one or two a week. A different type of port was introduced, and this port required a different needle. Therefore, before going to the ER to perform the procedure, I would ask the nurse to identify the type of port that patient had.

After approximately 15 years of serving as the Director of IV team, I was told that the team desired a director who would be available during the day. Alas, I was still on nights. The team members often had questions that they wanted immediate answers to at the time they were performing the patient care. I understood this need; I had felt it was not fair to either the team or me to have a director that worked the night shift. When I took the position, it was with the hope of soon assuming a full-time position as a unit director, as the DON had promised. Unfortunately, a couple years after I took on the extra duties as the Director of IV team, that DON left the hospital for another job. The outstanding promise had not been transferred to her replacement. I was still about ten years from retirement (or so I thought at the time), yet coming to the realization that I would most likely remain a night shifter until the end.

When the Director of IV team duties were given to a day shift director, I was relieved. I could focus better on my full duties as the night shift supervisor. Further, with additional paperwork requirements in my later years as supervisor, I was happy to forego the additional budgeting, policies/procedures, and scheduling for the IV team.

While I had taken on these duties with no extra salary, doing so actually resulted in a decrease to my salary. About five years after I had ended my duties as Director of the IV team, I was called in by the current DON and Personnel Director. They said, incorrectly, that I had been given extra salary for assuming the duties of the Director of IV team, and my salary had not been decreased when the duties were removed. My salary was now being reduced. This came at a time period when the hospital was firing personnel. Given my age, I knew it would be difficult to start over at another facility. It was clear to me that what they concluded was final, and not open to discussion. I felt like I had to accept this fallacy, in order to finish my career.

In another five years, the IV team would be dissolved. Shortly before I retired, under the policy of a larger network that the hospital had joined, all of the RNs were trained in starting IVs. During my last year and a half of full-time nursing, I was only called to start or restart the "difficult sticks." At that time, the RNs also had to administer the blood transfusions for their patients. We had gone full circle on this issue during my career. In my opinion, it was always preferable to have the patient's RN perform the blood transfusion. To me, this is part of the care the patient's RN should be able to perform. I had performed the blood transfusions on night shift for almost 30 years. Returning these duties to the RNs gave me more time for my administrative duties.

# CHAPTER 21

## *Cardiac Arrest Data*

Not long after I was given the IV team responsibilities, I sat at another supervisors' meeting where the DON was assigning additional administrative duties. I was wondering if any would fall to me, when the DON looked at me and simply directed, "And you are to collect monthly data on cardiac arrests." She explained the fields of information that she wanted on the monthly reports. This included the probable cause of each arrest, procedures implemented, any malfunction of equipment, whether the patient survived, and where they received care afterward (normally either our ICU or a hospital in Pittsburgh). It was up to me how to collect and present the data.

At the time, the hospital did not compile this particular data. So, there was no format for these statistics that I could use as a guideline. Therefore, I developed my own form, with the data the DON required, and additional fields to document the time, date, patients' medical record numbers (but not their names), and other event information. The information could, thus, be verified if necessary. If the patient survived, I included not only where they were treated thereafter, but if transported, the mode (ambulance or helicopter).

My main source for the info was the "Cardiac Arrest Record Sheets." At each arrest, one of the RNs at the code would be chosen to "scribe." If an inexperienced nurse was present, I usually gave this duty to her. Observing and recording would make her more comfortable at the next code. The scribing RN records the medications and time they are given, rhythms, shocks and voltage, and other data. She also records the underlying cause of the arrest, whether a heart attack, a respiratory arrest, trauma, overdose, or electrical shock. I asked each department, for all shifts, to send me a copy of each Cardiac Arrest Record Sheet. These were paper copies at the time; most were carbonless, and the ER's were machine copies. The copies were put in my mailbox in the supervisors' office, and I input this data into my monthly report. Initially, I handwrote this report, and a secretary typed it.

The problem with this early procedure for collecting the data was that staff often forgot to give me a copy of the sheet. Thus, to ensure I had an accurate monthly report, I found myself going through records and questioning staff. I would have to look through the ER's patient list each day to find the arrests. Then I would look through the code book at the front desk to see what codes had been logged for the month. Once I had my list, I would go to the medical records department and look up the patient's paper records, and then fill out my form. Thus, collecting the data could be time-consuming. When I had any extra time during my night shift, I would work on the data collection. Occasionally, I would come in early to do this.

I worked with this paper records system nearly all my career. Even when the nurses began typing their notes in the computer, the notes would be printed out and placed in the patient's chart. I later began typing the data into a computer form, which made the process easier.

Through this data collection, I did notice some interesting trends at our hospital. For example, when the use of Narcan became prevalent, there was a decrease in the number of cardiac arrests from overdoses treated at our hospital. Narcan, i.e. Naxolene, is a medication that is used to counter the effects of opioid overdose. It was usually given by first responders before the patient was brought to the hospital emergency room.

When I was given this extra duty at the supervisors' meeting, I had assumed it would be for only a short period, until the DON had the information she needed for whatever policy decisions were under consideration. I had this extra duty until I retired, 25 years later.

# CHAPTER 22

## *Halloween Trail*

"I can't see out of this head," I told my son. "You have to tell me what's happening." My son, dressed as Mickey Mouse, and assisting me in my volunteer work for the hospital, replied, "There's another group coming down the trail." The Minnie Mouse costume I was wearing had a huge head, and its opening for the eyes did not align with mine. The eye openings rested on my forehead. If I wanted to see out, I had to tilt the costume head and hold it in place, which was awkward. Fortunately, I could mostly just stand in place to play my part. I waved my hands at the sound of the approaching kids.

Prior to the strike, the hospital always had a full patient load, i.e. "census". In fact, as I mentioned, I often had to find a way to make a room for a new patient. After the strike, the hospital census dropped to approximately half. Even years later, it hadn't fully recovered. I understood why patients did not want to come to the hospital. A lot of people in the area belonged to unions and carried animosity toward the hospital, which they blamed for the strike. I also had people tell me that they were afraid to have the aides take care of them because of the strikers' angry words and manners on the picket line. The strike had high media attention. Having witnessed the strikers' behavior firsthand myself, I understood

158

their concerns. However, I replied, "Don't be concerned. We will take good care of you."

Several months after the strike, this issue of the low census was raised at a management meeting. We brainstormed the problem. This was not an issue of the breadth of medical care offered. We saw the issue, rather, as one of reconnecting with the community, reestablishing trust with them. We wanted to show we were there for and cared for the community and its families. Someone came up with the idea of a Halloween Trail for children in the community. We had the perfect spot for it. There was a one-mile walking path on the hospital property with fitness stations dispersed along the path. After much discussion, we said, "Let's do it!"

A committee was formed of managers and employees. With much excitement for our project, we discussed dates, security, decorations, costumes, treats for the children, and advertising. We decided to hold our event the week before Halloween so we wouldn't compete with traditional trick-or-treating. The trail would be for children up to twelve years of age, and they would be encouraged to wear costumes. It wouldn't be a scary trail, but fun, with staff volunteers dressed in costume to greet children and families and to provide treats. Employees donated the candy or money to help buy items. The family of one of the hospital workers owned an orchard, and that family donated our one healthy treat—apples. A snack manufacturer donated individual bags of potato chips and pretzels. We didn't know how many kids would come, but we prepared for several hundred.

For our first Halloween Trail, the hospital did not have any costumes or decorations in storage. We used whatever we had at home or borrowed from someone. We carved pumpkins, blew up balloons, and strung lights in the trees. Some volunteers brought appropriate music to play on a boom box at their stations.

The time for the event was set for 4:00 to 5:30 p.m. Many people arrived early. This was a promising sign. The line of people started forming a half hour before the start time. The children and accompanying adults were met at the start of the trail by clowns giving out trick-or-treat bags to those who did not bring their own. We discovered that a few of the children were afraid of the clowns. We pulled someone, costumed differently, from her station to greet these children.

The first year, I was stationed near the end of the trail. I waited with another nurse, ready to see the children. Word came down the line that the kids were on the way. I was hoping for a good turn out, and I was not disappointed. I do not recall my costume that year, but unlike in my Minnie Mouse costume, I had no problem seeing the kids. They seemed to be having a good time. I found out later that we had around 500 kids. To ensure we had enough treats for everybody, the managers in charge sent someone to the hospital to raid the snacks in the kitchen supply—chips, pretzels, cookies.

We were thrilled with the turn out. Seeing how happy the little ones were made it all worthwhile. Parents thanked us for doing the event. We told the parents that on trick-or-treat night, they could bring the children's treats up to the hospital and have them x-rayed free of charge. We offered this service for parents concerned that a malevolent person may implant a dangerous metal object in a treat.

When the event was over, we packed up our stations and headed to the hospital for warmth and pizza. We were all tired but felt great about how the event went. That night, everyone agreed that we should have the event again. Management concurred and the Halloween Trail became an annual event.

Each year, I took pleasure in choosing a new costume. Some of these belonged to the hospital, through either purchase or staff dona-tion. The Minnie and Micky Mouse costumes were the hospital's. Even though I could not see out of it, the Minnie Mouse costume was one of my favorites, because the kids loved it. Many wanted pictures taken with Micky and Minnie! My son, Allen, joined me a second year. Our station had a military theme. So, he wore Art's old sailor uniform, and I dressed as Betsy Ross, sitting in a chair with a flag in my lap. On other occasions, I joined other hospital workers for a group costume. I was the tin man in the Wizard of Oz group, and another year I was one of several witches around a cauldron filled with treats. The trail was a great project—not just for the kids—but for the staff as well. This creative endeavor, outside of routine hospital work, helped instill a family atmosphere and bonds between people in different departments.

Over the years, the number of children attending increased, growing to over 1,000. As the event grew, businesses in the community also donated items. The trail was a safe and fun place to bring the children. And, in my opinion, it did help mend the relationship between the hospital and the community.

# CHAPTER 23

## *"I want to speak to the Supervisor."*

When I saw who the patient was, I thought, "Here we go again." I was responding to the ER's page; a patient had demanded the supervisor. I first spoke to the ER nurse to get information on the reason for the patient's demand; I liked to be prepared. It was what I expected. The nurse explained that the patient claimed to be in severe pain, and the doctor would not give or prescribe anything stronger than Tylenol. It was 2016, and the doctor had checked the web-based pharmacy systems. The patient's records showed that she had two prescriptions filled the previous week at two different pharmacies. She had more than sufficient medication for standard dosages for pain relief. I had dealt with these situations before.

When I entered the patient's room, I recognized her from her many previous visits. I introduced myself (again) and said, "You wanted to speak to the supervisor." She said, "You'll help me." Her complaint mirrored her previous complaints. She wanted a particular pain medication. I listened to her complaint, and told her that I would speak to the doctor. I knew what the outcome would be, but still had to go through my response process . . . or at least pretend to. Now with Pennsylvania's online prescription data base, it was more difficult for a patient to obtain additional medications that were not medically merited. The doctor could see the frequency and amount of controlled substances recently dispensed to the patient. I walked over to the doctor's desk and noticed that the patient's husband had come into the hall and was watching me. I told the doctor that I was pretending to ask for additional pain medication for the patient, but I knew she couldn't have it. He simply confirmed, "No, she's not getting anything else." After a couple of minutes, I walked back into the patient's room. I explained in a kind but firm manner that she could not have anything stronger. I was frank with her. I told her that I knew she had prescriptions filled several days prior. She admitted she had, but said she needed more. Once she realized she would not get the prescription she demanded, she told me she would just go somewhere else. We notified the closest hospital that she may be coming and gave them a report.

Several times a week, I would be paged to respond to a patient or family member demanding to speak to "the supervisor." While there were many legitimate complaints that I was able to address, most of these complaints were from patients who did not like the constraints of their doctor's orders. In addition to the drug seeking patients, I would be called, for example, to speak to a patient who was angry that he could not have a cup of coffee before a test that required no food or drink after midnight. I found myself in a position repeating what the nurse had told him and offering him something to swab out his mouth if it was dry. On some occasions, I would explain additional ramifications. I might explain to the patient that if he had the cup of coffee, the test could not be performed and he would have to do it at a later date.

I would also be called to speak to patients who wanted to sign themselves out against medical advice. Certainly, they had this right, but I needed to explore the situation with them. It could be that the patient was mad that the medical procedures they desired had not been ordered. It could be a strong desire to return home or to resume daily responsibilities. It could even be a personality conflict with the nurse. Each situation was different, and I responded accordingly. Of course, if I could not convince them to stay, there was paperwork to be completed. Patients had to sign a document stating they were leaving against medical advice. Before the patients signed, I wanted to ensure they were not later surprised with the ramifications. I told them that the insurance company might not pay the hospital bill, given that they were signing out against medical advice. I further explained that if they waited until morning, when their doctor could see them, they could discuss with him or her their desire for discharge. Perhaps the doctor would agree. After hearing this, about half of these patients decided to wait until morning, and the other half signed and left.

Other situations I was called to were more complicated and required the supervisor's leadership. As a typical example, one night when I was getting a report from the evening shift supervisor, she told me of a situation that needed my attention. A patient on a med-surg unit was in serious condition, and the husband and children had requested her transfer to a large Pittsburgh hospital with more specialized equipment. The doctor agreed to the transfer and told the family that the patient needed a certain medication that could be provided in the larger hospital's ICU. This medication could not be provided on a med-surg floor. The family was upset that transfer arrangements were taking so long. I made a mental note to check on this patient first, but before I left the supervisor's office, I received a call from the nurse on that unit. She requested that I come up right away; the family was very upset and wanted answers from someone. I went straight up to the room and introduced myself. The patient was in bed unresponsive. There were approximately seven family members around her—the husband, children and the children's spouses. Several started yelling at me. I put up my hand and said, "Hold it!" They paused to listened. I said, "First, your mother can still hear you even if she isn't responding. So, let's keep the noise down. Second, I just came on shift and I don't know what has happened before I came on duty. So, *one person* update me." I looked at the husband to provide me information. He filled me in, and told me his wife needed a medicine but it could only be given in ICU, and the transfer to Pittsburgh was taking too long. I quickly checked his wife and told him I would be right back.

I went to the desk and asked the patient's nurse for a report. She informed me that we were waiting for a bed in the Pittsburgh hospital's ICU, and the patient would be transferred upon this notification. I asked her to call the doctor and get permission to transfer the patient to our ICU so the medication could be started before the bed in Pittsburgh was ready. I informed our ICU and the family of this plan. As soon as I received the doctor's okay, we transferred the patient to ICU and started the medication. I let the family go into the ICU to see her, two at a time, kept them informed and provided them drinks. The Life Flight crew stationed at our hospital was informed of the situation, and they were able to respond immediately when we were finally notified that Pittsburgh was ready for the transfer. When the patient was being taken out of ICU, I let the family stand in the hallway to see her once more before she was loaded onto the flight. The family came to me and thanked me for helping. The husband called me an angel. I knew I was only doing my job, but it was nice to know that my actions alleviated some of the family's distress.

On the other end of the spectrum, sometimes patients ask for the supervisor, because they just want to talk to somebody. One night I got a page from one of the med-surg units. When I answered it, I was told a male patient wanted to talk to the supervisor. I said, "I'm on my way," hung up the phone, and let out a long sigh. This man was frequently admitted to the hospital and he always needed to talk with the supervisor. When I went into his room, he started complaining that he had received his medicine ten minutes late. I explained that every patient can't receive their medications at the same time, to the minute. The nurse has a thirty-minute window to give them. He readily accepted that, but continued to talk. For the next twenty minutes I heard his life story which I had heard before. Then my pager went off. I told him I had to go answer it, and he should try to get some sleep. The page was for the floor I was on, so I walked to the nurses' station. When I asked them what they needed, one of the nurses said, "I just thought you needed a break from his talking." I sincerely thanked them; I had other things that needed my attention.

# CHAPTER 24

## *Family Experiences*

"Just do it, Ruth! Do it!" my colleague said. I was tempted. I could easily take the needle from the paramedic and insert it into a vein. My specialty. During the night shift, I started all IVs on the med-surg units. And when an ICU nurse experienced a difficult IV insertion, I would be paged. When I answered the page, I would hear, "Could you start an IV for us?" Can't start the IV? No problem, I'm on my way. Only, it was a different situation now.

I was well versed in the hospital's standards for medical professionals. My job was within the walls of the hospital. I was not an RN paramedic. It was out of bounds for me to start IVs in the field. I understood; no issue there. Now, however, with my 9-year old grandson sobbing in pain from a broken femur, and the paramedic unable to find a vein for pain medication, I must admit that the authority of the rules got a bit fuzzy for a moment. I wanted to take over for the paramedic.

Having unwisely accepted a double dog dare (another story), my grandson now lay at the base of a telephone pole, a bicycle damaged beyond repair next to him. He had biked down a steep curved hill with his friend's bike. Going at a high speed, he hit a support wire for a telephone pole. The pole happened to be in front of the house of a fellow nurse at the hospital. She called me to say, "Your grandson had a bad bike accident. We've called the ambulance." She told me where he was, and I ran around the block to him. I arrived at the scene the same time as the ambulance. My grandson lay on the ground sobbing. I did a visual assessment and could see that his left femur was broken. Before the paramedics reached him, I asked him questions to see if he had other injuries.

After doing an assessment, the paramedics attempted to administer the pain medication, via IV, but were unsuccessful. I was confident I could do it. I imagined directing the needle into his vein and his screams of pain diminishing. And I was urged on by a fellow nurse. "Come on, Ruth." Would the paramedics have even let me do the procedure, if I asked? They knew me as an RN. So, would they? I'll never know; I didn't ask. I let out a long breath and stepped back. I knew I had to let the paramedics do their job. There is solid reason behind the boundaries. I walked home for my car and followed the ambulance.

Like most families, mine has had its share of medical care, including emergency and ICU care. Viewing medical care from the recipient and family member's side brought me additional insight that I drew on throughout my nursing career. It is more than just the ability to empathize that I am speaking of. Obviously, empathy is a desired core attribute for nurses. Without it, nursing would have been just a job, not a calling, to me. However, in helping a family get through a medical incident, it is the manner in which that empathy is exhibited—the communication, the sharing of information—that I continually learned to improve on. And my experiences on the receiving side impacted my nursing approach. It was my husband's accident that left its deepest mark in this area.

Art lay in the ICU in a trauma hospital, about two hours from Canonsburg. He had suffered a severe head injury in a car accident, and he was now unresponsive and intubated. All my five children had come to the ICU, one from Africa where she was serving in the Peace Corps.

During the time we waited in the ICU waiting room, I received very little information from the doctor, nurses, or supervisor. In fact, I was surprised that the supervisor only spoke to me a couple times in the four weeks I was there. I realize that it was a large hospital and she had other duties, but I felt that she should have given more attention to the visitors in ICU, ensuring they understood the family's member condition and treatments. Likewise, the nurses in ICU rarely provided me valuable information. Normally, I was left to read the monitors, and interpret my husband's condition myself. There was one doctor who did, after my urging, provide me in-depth medical information. This was the radiologist who had interpreted the initial CT scan. I told him I wanted to see the scan myself. He said, "No, you really don't. It's not good." I insisted. "I need to know what we are dealing with." On the way to Radiology, he asked me again if I was sure I wanted to see the scan. When I confirmed, he showed me. The images showed extensive damage. The brain tissue appeared shredded and scrambled, especially in the frontal lobe. But I thanked him. He said, "You're a strong lady." I am a nurse; I had to know the facts. I truly appreciated that he respected my need for information. Not all doctors were as considerate.

In fact, one day, after Art had been in the ICU for a few days, a doctor came out in the waiting room, called my name and, standing several feet away from me, matter-of-factly said, "We are going to do a partial lobectomy tomorrow morning. He has to have this, or he will not survive. They'll bring you the papers to sign." And then he walked away. I was stunned. This was out of the blue and horribly communicated. This doctor explained nothing of the procedure or the expected permanent side effects, and I was not even given the opportunity to ask questions. Nonetheless, I signed the forms that were brought out to me later. In the procedure, to relieve pressure on Art's brain, the doctors removed part of Art's left frontal lobe. Because he was not expected to survive, they did not replace the piece of skull removed.

Given Art's current medical condition and the severity of his head injury, the children and I had the difficult but frank discussion of whether I should direct a no-code, meaning that Art would receive no life-saving treatment. At the end of the discussion, everyone was in agreement. It's what Art would have wanted. I signed the order. At this point, Art had been in the ICU for a week; we now knew of the severity of his brain damage, and his systems were beginning to fail. Even if he could survive given advanced medical treatment, we did not feel it was fair to him or the family to have him live in a vegetative or other severely diminished state. In Art's room, we played him Frank Sinatra and other of his favorite music. We talked to him, and gave him sports scores. We called a priest who administered last rites. My minister called me every day to see how I was doing and to receive updates on Art's condition. For good measure, when the Jewish Rabbi was in ICU, I was contented when he also visited Art.

I did not want any advanced medical treatment done, including resuscitation; I wanted Art to be comfortable in his last days. Not only did the medical professionals fail to communicate with me in any adequate degree, my no-code order was not followed to my intentions and my medical knowledge of the language. One morning, after I ordered the no-code, I walked into the ICU to see Art. A nurse and an intern were at his bedside. The intern was inserting a central line into an artery in Art's groin. The line was being directed toward his heart. They were preparing to give him blood. When they saw me, there was a shocked look on both of their faces. I asked them what they were doing. They explained that Art was bleeding internally and they needed to give him blood. I turned around and walked out. I should have said something, but was too upset and worn down by Art's condition. Even if I had *not* given the no-code, I would have expected them to seek my permission before performing this procedure. At Canonsburg Hospital, we definitely would have sought the consent of the appropriate family member before inserting a central line or giving a patient blood. And I was right there at the hospital; they knew I was there 24/7 for Art. No one asked for my consent, let alone informed me of the planned procedure. Apparently realizing the error, the head nurse soon came out to speak to me. She anticipated my complaint and began by explaining how they interpreted my no-code as only applying to CPR. This initial communication was revealing in that I had not even raised the issue yet. To me, they were violating my no code order. I explained that my interpretation of the no code, of the document I had signed, prohibited all advanced treatments, not just resuscitation. To this day, it is unbelievable to me that not one of the medical professionals thought to speak to the spouse, and get her consent, before performing the procedure.

Art was in ICU for another week, before he was transferred to another unit. By that time, he looked like a skeleton with skin over him. I lost a significant degree of respect for and trust in the staff. While the ICU had posted visiting hours, I no longer felt constrained by these. I needed to check on Art and get information for myself, as I could not trust the staff to inform me of his changing condition. One day, my youngest son, 13 years old at the time, went to tell his father the score of a football game (which I'm sure Art would have appreciated if he could understand). An ICU nurse reprimanded me because it was outside of visiting hours. After my experience with the staff, I was unapologetic. I told her, "His father is in there dying! If he wants to come in and tell him the score of a ballgame, he can do it!" She walked away.

After three months, Art came out of the coma, and had to relearn how to walk, talk, chew, swallow . . . basically everything. Art survived another 17 years, but in an extremely diminished state. I had to change nursing facilities several times due to his behavioral problems, uncharacteristic of the man I had married. I also changed nursing facilities due to subpar care. I initially selected a facility close to home for Art's post rehab care. That was a mistake; I discovered that they didn't know how to take care of head injured patients. Art was starting to have a decrease in awareness. When I visited, he would be strapped in a chair with head down, not observing anything. I found out that the staff was sedating him and strapping him in the chair for the day. He had a diaper on and was not taken to the toilet. I wrote a letter to the administrator and the Director of Nursing, telling them how upset I was with the care and that I would be sending him back to rehab as soon as I could make the arrangements. To this day, I will not recommend that facility to anyone. The care at some other facilities, however, was wonderful. At one facility, the staff interacted pleasantly with Art, gaining his favor when they bought him sandwiches and other treats and allowed him to eat at their desk as they observed him. For several years he was able to attend a cerebral palsy institute that improved his activities of daily living. Art had no short-term memory and very little long-term memory. I visited weekly, but he would not remember these visits, nor did he ever know my name. One day, he simply asked me, "Am I supposed to like you?" I replied, "Yes, you are." Because the piece of skull that was removed had not been replaced, he had a large depression on the left side of his forehead, which was an outward reminder to me of the severe damage he had incurred. I often find myself asking that what-if question—if my desires against advanced treatments had been followed, would Art have been spared 17 years of existing earthbound without really living?

Just nine months after Art's accident, my son Randy started having severe ear pain. He was nineteen. He went to the ER twice, and then to an ENT. He then had a procedure to drain fluid in the ear; but that was found not to be the issue. Randy then started to have severe joint pain to the point where he could barely move. He was finally diagnosed with a rare autoimmune disease, Wegener's granulomatosis, and was treated with steroids and chemotherapy. After a period of remission, the disease returned, and he started dialysis. He needed a kidney transplant. His younger brother, Allen, volunteered, and the two went through the necessary tests. Allen was a close enough match. Then as the boys were anticipating a call for a surgery date, the hospital called only to state that they had lost all the medical records. I have had my share of time searching in the records room for hardcopy records when the ER needed them stat, but I have never experienced a true loss of records. I was just as upset as my boys. The hospital told Randy that he and his brother would have to come back in and take the tests again. Randy thought hard about it, and decided he did not want Allen to give him a kidney, as Allen may need it later for a future son or daughter. Randy never received a transplant.

After Randy had been accurately diagnosed, he received appropriate care. Until he received his diagnosis, however, there were times that I felt he was judged by his looks—long hair, leather jacket, wallet chain. When he went in for severe ear pain, when no ear infection was apparent, perhaps they thought he was a drug seeker. I knew he was truly in severe pain. And Randy would not even take an aspirin.

Randy survived 20 years with the disease. I was working at the hospital when my grandson, Randy's son and namesake, called me to say his father was not breathing. He had called 911 and he and Randy's girlfriend were administering chest compressions, but they could not get Randy's mouth open. I hurried home. I arrived before the paramedics; the police were now administering CPR. Likewise, they could not get his mouth open, and had an oxygen mask over it. I asked if they were getting a reading; they replied no.

After Randy had been transported to the hospital, the doctor said he could not intubate Randy because his jaw was clamped too tight. He asked me if I wanted him to do a tracheotomy to insert a breathing tube. I said no; it had been too long. He was gone.

My own experiences have made me more aware of the families waiting at the hospital. I understand the need for acknowledgement and information. When supervising, I would go and speak to the family members, offer them coffee or tea. If I saw they were staying overnight, I asked if they needed a blanket or pillow. If they needed information regarding the patient's condition, I would talk to the nurse and bring an update to the family. When we had a critical patient, I would ask the nurses the code status of the patient. I would then check the chart to make sure all the paperwork had been properly signed. If anything was lacking, I would speak with the nurse to inform her of the missing information. If the family was at the hospital, I would also speak to them regarding their wishes and the necessary paperwork.

I became a resource person for families with head injured patients in ICU. Located about half a mile from our hospital was a rehab center with a unit for the head injured, and their patients were often admitted to our ICU. If family members arrived during the night, I would be called to speak to them. In addition to answering medical questions, I could also empathize on a personal level. I was able to talk with them about my experiences, and I knew what questions to ask. They seemed comfortable talking to someone who knew what they were going through.

As a nurse, it was sometimes difficult to find myself on the flip side of the coin as a family member arranging for the care of a loved one. I had to trust their care in the hands of other nursing personal. And to be honest, sometimes I was disappointed in what I saw and heard. Since Art could not speak for himself, I had to be his voice. For 17 years, I made sure I was informed of his care and I observed the interaction between him and the staff. There were a few times I felt the need to contact the Director of Nursing, and times I felt the need to find another facility.

I feel these experiences helped me to be a stronger person and a better nursing supervisor. As I flipped the coin back and forth between nurse and family member, I realized that for me both sides intersect each other. And I'm always a nurse no matter what side I am on.

# CHAPTER 25

## *New Ambulatory Care Center*

It was the day I would see the new ambulatory care center. I was excited at the idea of another expansion to the hospital, and I was especially looking forward to seeing this particular department. It was the department that I had designed bottom up 15 years ago, prior to construction of the new hospital. When I was designing the prior ambulatory care center, the hospital did not have one, and I had to piece together the expertise of others to ensure the facility would meet the department's needs. While I was pleased with the area I had designed and it was suitable for the hospital's anticipated needs, we had outgrown those needs. Now, with a fully functioning ambulatory care department, my input in the redesign was not needed. I had not seen any blue prints or walked through the area during construction. So, this was my first look at the design. I had high expectations.

I was not disappointed. The department was spacious compared to the smaller area it had replaced. Although it was attached to the main hospital, it had its own entrance and designated parking lot. Large letters above the department entrance read "Ambulatory Care." The entrance doors opened up to a waiting room and an area for the registration clerk.

There was also a table in a corner with coffee and tea for the families while they were waiting.

The ambulatory care center encompassed a doctor's office, two exam rooms, an endoscopy room, a colonoscopy room, a large recovery room, a room for patients receiving chemotherapy and blood transfusions, and a seven-bed section for patients having outpatient surgery. The latter section was where the outpatient surgical patients received both preoperative preparation and postoperative care. Surgeries were performed in the OR in the main area of the hospital. The nurses' stations and storage had ample space. The room for chemotherapy and blood transfusions was furnished with comfortable chairs and a TV; magazines were also provided. Little did I know that in a few years I would be bringing my mother-in-law to this room for her chemotherapy.

The Ambulatory Care Center generally closed around 5:30 p.m. and reopened early in the morning, prior to the close of my night shift. So, I would occasionally be called to obtain needed medications, such as a specific antibiotic that a doctor ordered to be taken pre-surgery. Other times, I would be called to perform a stat EKG on a patient prior to surgery. I was not prescheduled to do these; these were additional EKGs that the anesthesiologist requested immediately prior to surgery. While there was a technician to perform EKGs for these presurgical patients, that tech did not come on duty until 7 a.m. The page would always come around 6:30, while I was finishing my last round, getting ready to complete my shift paperwork. The phone number would tell me it was the Ambulatory Care Center. Responding to the page, I always hoped that it was just a request for a specific medication. Getting medications to this department took me about ten minutes. It took me twice as long to get the EKG machine, go to Ambulatory Care, perform the EKG, and clean and return the equipment.

Also, there were times that the center's equipment was used for an ER patient needing an endoscope ("endo") at night. Thus, I was given an additional duty. It was determined that if a patient needed an endo during night shift, the supervisor would assist with the procedure.

About twice a month, someone would come to the ER with something stuck in their throat—usually a piece of food. These patients were still able to breathe on their own, but needed medical intervention to clear the blockage. If the ER doctor could not remove it, he would have the on-call gastroenterologist summoned to perform the endoscopy. This is a non-surgical procedure, performed while the patient is under short-acting anesthetic, to examine a person's digestive tract. With the endoscope, a flexible tube with a light and camera attached to it, the doctor is able to view and move the material lodged in the esophagus. In addition to calling the gastroenterologist, the ER would also page me. In turn, I would then phone the ambulatory RN on call to come in.

After the ambulatory RN had set up the endo room, I would help take the patient there. The first time I assisted in an endo procedure, I told the ambulatory RN that she would have to tell me what she wanted me to do. My primary duties that first day were basic—watching the monitors and providing supplies. Although these duties were well within my professional capabilities, I was uneasy at first. I had never participated in an endo procedure, let alone observed one until that day. Further, I did not know where their supplies were located. After that first endo, I assisted with many others, and often had additional duties such as holding the patient's head in a certain position or suctioning the patient. Once started, the endoscopy usually took twenty to thirty minutes. It was interesting to watch the process on a screen. After the procedure, I would return the patient to the ER where he or she would be observed for at least an hour before being discharged. From start to finish, I was unavailable to perform other duties for up to one hour.

While we did not perform many endos on the night shift, over time, I got to know the very different personalities of the gastroenterologists. When the ER informed me of a needed endo, I would ask them which doc was on call. One of them had a rather rough bedside manner. I cringed when he gratingly reprimanded an adult patient, suffering already, to "chew his food" in the future.

Before we started an endo, I would let the front desk know where I was and directed them to hold all my calls. I always worried that there would be a code called during that time. I would not be able to leave the endoscopy room. I never thought supervisors should be unavailable for significant periods of time. The other night shift supervisor held the same opinion. So did the 3-to-11 supervisors. During day shift, the Ambulatory Care Center was fully staffed. At a supervisors' meeting, we raised the issue with the Director of Nursing. We explained that we had to be available to attend all codes and emergency situations. It was not desirable for us to be tied up for thirty to sixty minutes on non-supervisory duties. The DON assured us she would bring our concern to the administration, and she did. We did not get the answer we had hoped for, and continued to assist in the endos.

One night I entered the supervisors' office to receive the shift-change report from PT. She was always relaxed but professional. She told me that a patient needed an endo, and she had already phoned the on-call ambulatory nurse. She laughed, "She'll be coming in soon, and you'll have to help. It's your turn. I'm out of here."

# CHAPTER 26

## *Time to be a Daughter*

"But I don't like water." It was the mid-90s and my mother, now frail, was at risk of another urinary tract infection. Her doctor had told her she needed to drink more water, and I repeated the direction to her many times. When one of my brothers visited, he sought to remedy the situation with a water softener device that attached to the kitchen spigot. After installing the device, he told our mother that the water would now taste better. She thanked him for the water softener. After he left a couple days later, she confided in me, "I still don't like the water." I bought her lemonade and cranberry juice, which she drank some of but not as much as I had hoped.

I was blessed with a kind and gentle mother. During her younger years, she was very active. She worked full time in a dress shop a short walk from our house. When I was in school, we always had lunch together. I would walk home from school and she would walk from the dress shop. She would make lunch for us, and we would watch a soap opera together, *Search for Tomorrow.* The episodes ran only 15 minutes then. I have good memories of those times, just my mom and me, eating and commenting on the soap opera. In the evening, after dinner, she would play the piano, and my father and I would sing. She was also involved with two fraternal organizations, Eastern Star and the Pythian Sisters. For the latter, she was the Grand Chief of Pennsylvania for a year. I did the typing for her speeches and agendas. She was also a deacon in our church, taught Sunday school, and led a senior high youth group. At home, in addition to being a mother, she took care of my grandmother, who lived in the same house with us. She canned fresh vegetables, grown by her sisters. I recall them all together, the three sisters and my grandmother, with baskets of vegetables and fruits, chopping and chatting. My mother also made a prolific amount of baked goods. When she got home from work and had no other commitments, she would start baking—cookies, doughnuts, cakes. We always had cookies in our house—for tea, a bedtime snack, or to share with visitors. In the 1990s, as my mother's energy and physical ability diminished, there came a time when she had to buy cookies from the grocery store so we would have them available for tea. The first time she brought store-bought cookies into her house, she was extremely apologetic to me. I decided then that I better bake some cookies myself.

My father had died in 1987. My mother, now alone in her house, was afraid that she would die and no one would find her in a reasonable time. She wasn't afraid of death, however. In fact, she looked forward to being reunited with my father. She would say, "Why doesn't God take me?" Her fear was simply that no one would discover her body until long after she had died. There was no reason for such concern. I lived a mile away, and was at her house daily. I also drove her to events at church and lodge. A friend of hers took her five times a week to the senior citizens center in town. Yet, I complied with her request to call her every morning when I got home from work.

I was at her house every afternoon. When I did not have any day-time meetings at the hospital, I would usually sleep from 9:00 a.m. to 1:00 p.m. After I got up, I did some chores or studying and then went to her house for about an hour. We would have tea and cookies, talk and watch TV. Later, I would call her before I went to bed for my evening sleep. I slept about 8:00 p.m. to 10:00 p.m., and then got up to get ready for work. For several years, this schedule worked well for checking on my mother.

In the mid-90s, I started noticing my mother's weight diminishing. She had always been a petite woman but had gotten down to 100 pounds. While she fixed her own meals, I didn't think she was getting enough nourishment. I would question her on what she had for dinner. Sometimes, she merely made toast. So, when I made dinner for my sons and me, I made extra for her and brought it to her house in the early evening. After doing chores or errands or classwork, I would return once more to her house mid-evening to get her ready for bed. Then I would go home and take a quick nap before work. On Wednesday when I went to class at the University of St. Francis, I would leave her a milkshake in a bowl of ice. I would instruct her that she had to drink it all before I got back. Although she usually went to bed at 7:30 p.m., she would try to stay up for me until I returned from my class, closer to 10:00 p.m. Sometimes I would find her asleep on the couch, and I would get her into bed.

My routine now included three trips to my mother's house to take care of her, in addition to phone calls. It was difficult watching her decline. Sometimes, she would become confused. One time she looked right at me and said, "Ruth Ann is coming over soon." Seeing her condition, I did not try to explain to her who I was. I just said, "Okay." I took her to doctor appointments, and I called the ambulance when she needed immediate higher-level care.

In 1996, she was getting weaker and not able to do much. She asked me to promise to keep her in her home. I could not give her a very solid answer, because I did not want to make a promise I may not be able to keep. I told her, "Okay, Mom; I know you want to stay in your house." I intended to try to do this for her, but knew I was going to need more help than I alone could give her. I hired a young woman, who was recommended by another nurse. It was a very good recommendation. This woman was a blessing. From 8:00 a.m. to 2:00 p.m., she would wash and dress my mother and feed her breakfast and lunch. I continued to come to my mother's house three times a day—around 3:00 p.m. for afternoon tea and cookies, for dinner, and later in the evening to put her to bed. At one point, my mother stopped eating the dinners I made. When I asked her about it, she claimed that she did not like them. Both the aide I hired and I starting feeding my mother by hand, like a baby. At one point, I started using baby food because she did not like to chew. I would select meats and vegetables I thought she would like, and also made homemade applesauce. I was still determined to keep her at home, as she desired.

On one occasion, my mother did not answer when I called her in the morning. Apparently, she could not find the phone that was next to her. So, I started stopping at my mother's house after work, to check on her. A couple mornings, I found her on the floor by the bed. Both times, she indicated she had fallen on the way to the bathroom. On these occasions, I was able to dress her in her nightgown and get her to bed. On another occasion, however, I had more difficulty. I was walking her from the couch to her bed, when she went straight down. I could not catch her in time. She could not raise herself, and although she was less than 100 pounds, I could not lift her, as she could not assist. I knew that the neighbor across the street was in his yard, so I went out on the porch and called to him. He came right away, lifted her like a small child, and carried her to her bed. I was very grateful. I wondered how long I could or should keep my quasi promise to my mother.

In the spring of 1998, my mother had some trouble breathing so I called the ambulance, and explained to my mother that she had to go to the hospital. She was admitted, and after a few days the doctor told me she would have to have continuous oxygen. As soon as he said that, I knew it was time to find a nursing home. I told the doctor that I felt my mother needed to be placed. He looked at me and said, "It's about time you started being a daughter instead of her nurse."

I told mom she was only going to go to the nursing home until she got stronger. I knew I was not being honest, but she accepted that explanation. After she had been there three months, I could tell my mother had given up. She died that September. She was a special person and I was blessed to be her daughter.

# CHAPTER 27

# *Patient Privacy*

"Hello. This is Ruth. I'm the supervisor. You wanted to talk to me."

"I'm calling from Florida. I'm Betty Meyer's son. I need to know her condition. The nurses won't give it to me."

"I'm happy to help you, but you need to provide me the password. Do you have it?"

"No, I do not. But I am her son. I have a right to know her condition."

"I'm sorry, but I can't give you any information without the password. Why don't you get the password from your family, and then I can give you information."

"I don't talk to my family!"

"Well, I'm sorry, there is nothing I can do then."

After he replied with a few nasty words, he slammed the receiver. It was 1999, and the hospital had made significant changes with respect to privacy of patient information. This was in compliance with the Health Insurance Portability and Accountability Act (HIPAA) enacted by Congress in 1996. Congress felt there was a need for privacy and security standards especially with the increased use of electronic technology.

Prior to HIPAA, the nurses essentially trusted the caller to be who they said they were, and provided general information on conditions of family members. While we would not provide specifics on a patient's condition, we would say, for example, whether the patient was stable. We might also say that the patient had injured a leg or was going in for testing the next day. If the family member wanted to talk to the doctors, we would leave a note with a phone number on the patient's chart. Additionally, a visitor walking past the nurses' station might be able to read a patient's name on a chart. Patients' last names were printed on a long white sticker that was put on the side of the folder containing their chart. The folders were placed on a shelf behind the nurses' station, and when the doctors were making rounds, they would leave the charts on the ledge of the nurses' station with new orders. Anyone could read the names.

I first received instruction on HIPAA at a nurse managers' meeting. I realized that this law would require a significant change in how we handled information. I ran through my mind the changes we had to make. These would be significant. At first, my concern was strictly compliance with the law, but after implementing appropriate rules, I experienced a shift in mind set. I starting asking myself whether I would want my health care information available to the same extent patient information had been in the past.

We made the changes. Replaced by room numbers, the names came off the charts. All names were erased from the white boards. When a patient was admitted, the patient or a family gave us a password. Anyone calling in for information had to have the password, which we kept in the cardex. Even staff members were prohibited from accessing electronic files of patients that were not under their care. Once a staff member told me that she had seen that a certain person was in the ER and wanted to know if I expected that patient to be admitted. In lieu of telling her what I knew of the patient, I reminded her she was not allowed to access the ER system. It was up to me to tell the staff when and if they should expect a patient. No one was allowed to look at a patient's chart or records in the computer unless they were taking care of that patient. We were informed that we couldn't go into the computer and look at our own records. I had to go through my doctor for my own lab results. In the past, I could access my results on the hospital system.

While it took some effort to make these changes, we were diligent in implementing them. We were inspected by both state authorities and the Joint Commission on Accreditation of Healthcare Organizations. Compliance with HIPAA was examined as part of the inspection. As supervisor, I had to be observant to ensure we complied.

It took a few years for the public to become knowledgeable of these standards and how they were implemented. In the meantime, my staff and I handled many irate phone callers trying to get information on family members. I tried to help people as much as I could, within the law. I would check to see if the patient was awake or asleep. If the patient was awake and agreed to talk with the person, we would have the call transferred to their room.

I understood the frustration of the family members. As a wife, I had my own experience with HIPAA restrictions. One night, while I was at work, I had a phone message from the nursing facility where my husband was admitted. I was informed that Art had been transferred to the emergency room at another hospital. Unfortunately, this was not an exceptional occurrence. Art had difficulties with aspiration pneumonia. I called the emergency room where he was. I asked to speak to his nurse. I told the nurse who I was and that I was at work and unable to leave. I asked him about Art's condition. He said, "You know I can't give that to you." I knew the rules, but I needed information. Due to Art's diminished mental state, he could neither create nor communicate a password. I was his guardian but in a problematic position, not being able to obtain information. I said that I wanted to know the changes in his condition. The nurse put me on hold. When he came back, he said that he did not know Art's "normal condition." So, I described to him Art's normal condition.

He then said simply that Art was "not normal" that evening. I was grateful for that much information, albeit extremely limited. I reminded the nurse that Art was a "no code," and he said they were aware of that. I had a full shift ahead of me, and had no information to discern whether Art's condition warranted me trying to get a replacement supervisor mid-shift rather than visiting him in the morning. I simply had no idea how serious his condition was. So, I decided to give his nurse the hospital phone number and told him that he could call me with any questions. I said I would be over to see Art in the morning. I assumed that if Art's condition became more critical, they could call me, and I would find a replacement on no notice. I worked my shift with no knowledge of my husband's condition. I certainly understood the reasons for HIPAA but when I needed information, it was frustrating having the needed information withheld from me.

Phone calls from family members continued. A few years later when our hospital had joined a network, the staff and I sometimes felt that the "family members" calling were actually personnel from the network testing our compliance. When they failed to provide the password, we gave our standard suggestion that they contact their family to obtain the password. These callers were very polite and, in lieu of pressing the issue, they would say, "Thank you. I will talk to my family tomorrow." I reminded staff to never give out medical information to anybody that did not have the correct password.

# CHAPTER 28

## *Into the Next Millennium*

"Happy New Year!" I heard this from everyone as I made my first rounds. I usually worked New Year's Eve so the other supervisors could be with their families. But this one was a special one as it was December 31, 1999, on the edge of the new millennium. We had been preparing for this night for weeks with meetings and updates from the IT Department. We discussed the "Y2K" issue, the concern that some systems were not programmed to read the year 2000 correctly and may exhibit errors or fail altogether. In fact, we were told to prepare for a widespread computer crash at midnight. IT informed us that there was no remedy for preventing the issue, but they would try to fix it should it occur. We were told to have a back-up of paper supplies for charting, physician orders, and lab requisitions. As supervisor, I took the concern seriously, and ensured we had sufficient supplies on hand. These were the same paper supplies that we kept in the event of a power outage.

Given these concerns, an IT tech was on hand that night. Additionally, three of the nurse managers also were present for the transition to year 2000. They came in with their husbands and were in the dining room on North. Not the best locale to ring in the new millennium, but we all had Y2K concerns, and these managers wanted to be at the hospital in case there were any problems on their units. We all watched the clock. 11:45, 11:50, 11:55 . . . . Many patients had their TVs on, and nurses joined them to watch the events. I watched from ICU. If the computers crashed, patient care would be compromised in ICU and telemetry, as patients were on computer-run monitors. I was ready for hands-on care, if needed. In New York City's Time Square —the same time zone as Canonsburg—the ball started to drop. We held our breath. The countdown came and went, the crowd in Times Square cheered, and Auld Lang Syne was played. And our computers simply kept going, moving into the 21st century oblivious to the great anticipation that they would crash. In ICU, we toasted with sparkling grape juice. When I did my rounds, it appeared that each unit had similarly celebrated.

The year 2000 brought a significant change to our hospital. We became part of a larger health network, West Penn Allegheny Health System (WPAHS). We were still a nonprofit hospital that strived to have a positive balance sheet, but the Health System would now oversee our operations. I was expecting a change in this direction; I was only surprised that it had taken as long as it did. Back around 1980, a nurse manager and I went to Chicago to attend a conference on efficient running of hospitals. The conference was hosted by a large hospital, and the agenda included both traditional conference instruction as well as a moderated tour of the large hospital. To this day, I remember one particular moment of the conference. The instructor spoke to attendees who came from smaller hospitals. "Who here is from a small hospital?" My colleague and I raised our hands. He then said, "Small hospitals will not survive in the future unless they become part of a larger health system." At the time, Canonsburg Hospital (still in the old facility) was doing fine, and I thought I'll just have to wait and see how the future goes. The future that was predicted at that conference in 1980 was now here.

Soon after we joined WPAHS, I saw several advantages to being part of this larger network. First, in addition to the on-call pharmacist for Canonsburg Hospital, we now had another resource to contact. West

Penn Hospital had an on-duty pharmacist working the night shift, and we could call her if we had a question. I didn't have to wake up our pharmacist unless it was necessary. Also, there were a few times I needed a patient medication that we didn't carry in our pharmacy. I could now call West Penn and if they had it, they would send it out to me via courier. Previously, if our hospital did not have the needed medication, the doctor would change the prescription to an equally effective medication that we did have in stock or, if there was none, we would transfer the patient to another hospital.

Another benefit of the network was the monthly nursing management conference calls that were led by the nursing administration of West Penn and Allegheny hospitals. I usually called in from home. However, when these calls overlapped Canonsburg Hospital's own nursing management meetings, we telephoned in as a group from our hospital. The calls were informative—usually about new policies, procedures, changes in the hospitals. These calls kept us updated and we didn't feel left out of the loop. Another benefit was the translation resource. People of different nationalities, mostly Spanish speaking, were moving into our local area. Our hospital had a list of employees who could speak a second language, but at night it was hard to get hold of them. If the patient didn't have someone with them to translate, it was difficult to communicate. We had picture cards, but that didn't always work well. For example, we had cards that showed a face in pain and various body parts. Through these cards, we tried to get the patient to tell us where the pain was. One night the ambulance brought in a man who was found lying on the ground by the railroad tracks. He didn't speak any English. We called the translator line for the health system and someone was available to talk to him. Without the help of the larger system, the staff would not have been able to effectively communicate with the patient.

After we joined the health system, we were able to redesign and replace the skilled nursing unit with another type of care that would be less financially draining on the hospital. When in 1981 we received permission to build the new hospital, it was with the condition that it had a skilled nursing unit. So, from 1983 through 2000, we operated this unit on 2-North. However, Medicare had recently lowered its reimbursement rates, which meant that our skilled nursing unit was not profitable anymore. A decision was made to close the unit and turn it into a rehab unit. While the hospital had a physical therapy department on the first floor for both inpatient and outpatient care, we intended to expand this department. We desired to redesign 2-North for inpatient rehab as well as occupational therapy, and use the current physical therapy space on the first floor for strictly outpatients. We had to go back to the state licensing agency. Permission was granted. Working with the patients and family members, we found rooms in nearby facilities for our skilled nursing patients.

The skilled nursing unit was closed down and construction started. Occasionally, I would peek in the unit as construction progressed. A few times, I found a painter working late at night. I would introduce myself, and tell him I was just checking on the progress. In May 2000, the new rehab unit reopened. The two-bed skilled rooms were now large single-bed rooms. The rooms were bright and cheerful. The unit quickly filled up with patients not only from our hospital but also from other hospitals. Most patients came following orthopedic surgery, strokes, and head injuries. I enjoyed seeing how these patients progressed during their stay. One reason I had chosen the nursing profession was because I desired to be involved in improving the overall health of people. It was very rewarding to see these rehab patients improve.

A few years later, WPAHS introduced an interesting and time-saving addition to our ER. In 2005, each hospital received a "Tug," a mobile robot designed to make deliveries. In our hospital, Tug was used to bring patient specimens from the ER to the lab. Therefore, Tug had a station in the ER, where it recharged. Tug stood about chest high to me, and had a shelf protected by a door. It was programmed to exit the ER, go down the hall to the lab, open the door electronically, enter the lab, and announce that a delivery had arrived. The lab tech would remove the specimen and push a button for Tug to return to the ER. After returning to the ER, it would redock at its station. Tug was a very valuable "employee." Prior to Tug, a nurse had to walk the specimen to the lab, whenever the nurse had available time. Often, I would do so. Therefore, the specimens were not always taken to the lab immediately, but according to staff availability. With Tug, the specimens were sent immediately to the lab, thus, hastening the lab results. Tug attracted a lot of attention from patients and visitors, especially children. In the winter, one of the staff would dress Tug with a Pittsburgh Steelers knit cap or Santa hat. I would even catch myself saying "Hi, Tug," as I passed him in the hall. Then I would think "I'm talking to a robot!"

In a few months, Tug had to be reprogrammed when we opened a new larger ER. We had outgrown the original ER that we thought was so big in the beginning. The new emergency room had more than twice as many patient beds, with two rooms designated for critical care beds. There were two entrances—one for ambulances and one for walk-in patients. We soon saw an increase in the number of patients coming to the ER. Due to the increase in patients, additional staff was added.

During this time, I saw another shift in the drugs used by many patients being admitted to the ER. When we first moved to the new hospital, we would see ER patients with symptoms mimicking a heart attack; these patients would inform the doctor that they had used cocaine. This is in addition to the continuing number of patients with effects of marijuana use—which we had seen for years—often brought in by police who needed to ensure medical clearance before the person was incarcerated. And of course, patients with alcohol poisoning or addiction were always prevalent on night shift. After cocaine, the next wave I saw was heroin. While we did not have the volume of overdoses as the larger Pittsburgh hospitals, we had our share for a small community. When unresponsive patients were brought to the ER, we first checked their breathing. If they were breathing, we put them on oxygen, started an IV, and drew blood for tests ordered by the doctor. These tests would always include a drug screen. If the patient was not breathing, we would intubate and start CPR. Several of these patients who had used heroin did not survive. Upon each of these sad occurrences, the ER called the family. By the phone, the family was told only that the family member was in our ER, was critical, and they needed to come immediately. It was only after their arrival that the doctor would inform them that the patient did not survive. Many of these patients were young, and meeting with the parents was heartbreaking. We would clean the body and dim the lights, before I brought the parents back to see their child. However, if an autopsy was required or a death certificate had not yet been signed, we could not take out the endo tube or IV line. So, I had to prepare the parents for the condition of the body. This was part of nursing, but even after decades of nursing it remained difficult, especially with a young patient. I saw a full range of emotions over the years—crying, fainting, anger, denial. One mother insisted we were lying to her and her son was just sleeping. I tried to show sympathy and kindness, but still had to be honest with the tragic facts. I would explain to the family that they would have to make arrangements. I would walk them through the process. One night, a few days after I returned to work after my son Randy's death, we had a young man in his early twenties overdose. I was one of nurses working on him in the ER; we could not revive him. The family was called. Before they arrived, the doctor, who knew of my recent loss, looked at me and said, "When I heard the patient was being transported, I was so hoping you weren't on tonight."

Years later, when the use of Narcan (naloxone) become prevalent, I saw a drop in overdose deaths. In 2014, Pennsylvania state legislation allowed emergency personnel to administer this medicine, which blocks and reverses the effects of opioids. The first time I witnessed the administration of Narcan, I was amazed. Someone had dropped off an unresponsive patient at the ER and then took off. We had no information about the patient. The doctor suspected a drug overdose, and ordered an injection of Narcan. The ER nurse gave the injection, and within seconds the patient responded. He sat up, yelled, moved his arms and legs violently, and repeatedly threw up. We saved his life, but he was angry that we had stopped his buzz. With the use of Narcan by first responders, I saw not only a decrease in overdose deaths, but a decrease in unresponsive patients being brought to the hospital.

With the increase in patient load in the ER overall, we also saw an increase in the need for the Life Flight helicopter to transfer patients into Pittsburgh. At that time, we had a helipad but not a helicopter positioned at Canonsburg Hospital. Life Flights from Allegheny Hospital in Pittsburgh would land at Canonsburg Hospital to transport patients. After data analysis, it was determined that a helicopter should be stationed at Canonsburg 24/7. Not only would this result in quicker patient transport, but the helicopter at Canonsburg would also be closer to many of the car accidents where Life Flight was needed. A trailer was placed on the hospital grounds near the helicopter, so the crew had a place to stay while on duty. Before they took off or landed, the crew would notify security, who would perform vehicle traffic control in the immediate area. Each time I hear the helicopter fly over my house, I wonder what the medical issue is and I say a prayer for the patient.

We had other changes at the hospital during this period. A visitor lounge on the second floor was converted into a small sleep lab. It was one room with two patient beds, separated by a curtain, and a technician area. The room was near the stairs, used by staff. Thus, unfortunately, sounds from opening and closing doors could be heard in the sleep lab. The sleep lab tech monitored the sleep patterns of patients with sleeping problems, such as potential sleep apnea. Even after working night shift for so many years, I was surprised at the high percentage of people with sleep problems. Electrodes were connected to the patients prior to sleeping, so their brain patterns and vital signs could be monitored. The patients usually came in at 9 p.m. and left at 6 a.m. The 3-to-11 supervisor would let me know if there were patients in the sleep lab. I always wanted to know who was in the hospital at night; that was part of my job. On a few occasions, the sleep lab technician would call me to check a patient who was having health issues, such as a patient complaining of chest pains or nausea, or a patient with possible blood sugar issues. I would then take the patient to the ER to be checked. After several years in this location (the old visitor's lounge), the sleep lab was moved to the old ER which had been remodeled. There were now two private rooms with nicer beds, and a separate room for the technician with up to date equipment. The new sleep lab was in an area off to itself, thus much quieter. This was an excellent use of the old ER that was just being used for storage. I quietly went in the sleep lab each night it had patients and checked with the technician to see if everything was okay.

Along with the many changes in the hospital's facilities, a significant policy change was implemented. No smoking in the hospital! WPAHS had prohibited smoking within all their hospitals. Prior to this, staff smoked in designated lounges, and patients and their visitors smoked in the patient's room unless the patient had oxygen running. Looking back, this was so unhealthy. And in a hospital! After smoking was banned inside the hospital, I would sometimes be paged about a patient smoking in the room. I would go and talk with the patient. He or she usually denied it, but I would say, "I can smell it." Sometimes, if I could not trust the patient to follow the no smoking rule, I would lock the cigarettes and lighter in the patient's medication drawer until he or she was discharged. Later, I would ask the incoming 7-to-3 shift to request the doctor to order a NicoDerm patch for the patient. Alternatively, if a patient was able, a nursing assistant could take the patient to an outdoor patio to smoke.

I understand the need to smoke. My son Randy was told not to smoke when he became ill with a chronic illness. He cut way back but would still have one or two cigarettes a day. He said it eased the pain and helped him relax a little. After the new policy was implemented, the hospital built a smoking shack outside and to the left of the employee entrance. It had three sides with a roof and was equipped with benches. Employees also stood on the sidewalk or sat on the curb to smoke. When

I had to come in for a meeting in the afternoon I had to walk through the smokers. When they went back inside you could smell the smoke on them. I was glad I had given up smoking—a habit initiated from a sample provided at the cafeteria in South Side Hospital—years ago.

# CHAPTER 29

# *PT*

Over my long career, I have worked with hundreds of staff. There are those that I could never forget. They've left an impression on my life. They've made me laugh, we've shared personal stories, and they performed their job with the highest professionalism. These people created an ambiance that increased the enjoyment of my job. There was Robin at the front desk, performing switchboard and admission duties at night. Because she was the only person in her position, I would have to relieve her for her breaks. We shared food and stories, and together we experienced the many changes in the hospital over the years. By the time I retired, she was one of the decreasing number of staff who could "remember when" with me. There was Joyce—the ICU nurse with whom I drove to master's classes, the one who had enough persuasion to convince me to pierce my ears. There were many others. And among my fondest memories, there was PT.

PT was one of a kind. She was kind and compassionate, always smiling. Her matter-of-factness was combined with humor. You knew she was a nurse from the "old school" with her white uniform, white nursing shoes, and starched cap. At Canonsburg Hospital, she was the last nurse that I saw wearing the nursing cap. She wore her cap well into the

2000's, even after I had foregone mine. And under her cap, her bleached blonde hair was perfect. It was off the collar, pushed back on the sides, professionally teased. She always looked like she had just walked out of the beauty salon.

Nursing was not just a job to her, it was a calling. She felt a personal responsibility to the patients. She strived for the highest level of care and kept open communication with patients and their families. Sometimes staff would go to the funeral home for the viewing of a patient who had died. I would often go to support the families that I had gotten to know during the patient's stay. PT seemed to go to more viewings than the rest of us combined. She felt the need to show her respect. The supervisors and nurse managers would sometimes good-naturedly tease her about the frequency of her funeral home visits. If she came with a purse, for example, someone would say, "I see you have your funeral purse with you. Whose funeral did you go to this time?" The staff loved her.

For more than twenty years, PT was the 3-to-11 supervisor, from whom I took shift change. Mary Lou was the relief for both of us. We three worked well together. If one of us needed a certain day off, we would change the schedule to make it happen.

PT was not only an asset to the supervisors' office but she was a great friend. We talked about our families as well as hospital business. She had four children and I had five. She used to say that I snuck one in on her. Her boys were tall and thin as were mine. She would bring me jeans when her boys outgrew them, because they would fit mine. Her husband made delicious breads and she always made sure I got some.

One day in early 2007 she announced that she was going to retire. She said she had had enough! She was too professional to tell us what exactly brought her to her decision. I knew I would miss her, but I planned to always stay in touch. The supervisors and nurse managers took her out for a retirement lunch, where we laughed as we shared stories of her.

Shift change was not the same after she retired. I missed seeing PT with her perfect hair, chatting a little bit about our families, and laughing with her. She had a way of making administrative difficulties humorous even if they weren't. It was as if the sun had gone down.

A few months after PT retired, I took two nearly back-to-back vacations to visit family out of state and worked a couple days between trips. Mary Lou was working 3-to-11 the first night I came back between trips, however, she was not in the supervisors' office when I arrived. I was told she was in ICU, so I went down and greeted her. She said she had to tell me something. I thought it was about a patient, and was business-ready for whatever she had to tell me. I followed her to the kitchenette area, and was not prepared for what she told me. "PT died." I couldn't believe it. This was so sad. I was further saddened when I realized that I wouldn't be there for the funeral the upcoming week. Mary Lou said that PT had been hospitalized, but seemed to be doing well. Having been on vacation, I did not even know she had been admitted. Mary Lou further explained that she had spoken to PT before her death. PT was to be discharged the next day, and was anxious to go home to start preparations for cooking for Memorial Day weekend. Her death was unexpected. After hearing this news, I knew I had to get on with my shift but my heart wasn't in it.

When I returned from my next vacation, I found out that the hospital was going to have a memorial service for PT. I was comforted that I would be able to attend and visit with her family. The staff donated a plaque in her honor, and it was hung on the wall near the nursing units. I was proud to have worked with PT and proud to call her my friend.

# CHAPTER 30

## *Night without Power*

I was in the supervisor's office finishing my initial paperwork, when the lights went out. It was shortly before midnight. No problem, I thought, the hospital's generators will soon kick in. As all hospitals, Canonsburg Hospital had sufficient back-up power for such events. The staff was unfazed; it was more of a nuisance than a concern. As expected, the generators soon kicked in. My first step was to inform the front desk switchboard operator to contact the on-call maintenance personnel. When the hospital was operating under generator power, it was hospital policy to have maintenance present. At that time, maintenance did not work the night shift. I spoke with Robin at the front desk; she already had the number and was ready to place the call. Then, I started my rounds, and given the interruption in the electrical power, I intended to make sure all the computers and heart monitors were back up. I went through the ER. All good there. Then made my way down the hallway to intensive care. Again, all good.

I continued to the med-surg floors. The second floor was having some trouble getting the heart monitors back up. I informed the nurses to call the emergency customer service line for the monitors, and have them troubleshoot. With my walk-through complete, I took the stairs down with the intention of beginning one more walk through starting on the first floor. I preferred the stairs over the elevator, and was in the stairwell when the lights went off a second time. I reached for the railing and waited for the lights to come back on. Not only did the hospital have generators, it had back-up generators. So, I was surprised when, after a minute, the lights had not come back on. I carefully descended the stairs in the dark. I had a flashlight in my office, but had to get there first. On the first floor, I slowly walked the dark hallway to the front desk. Security was there, with a flashlight. I asked Robin if she had reached the on-call maintenance personnel. She said, "He's on his way." Security walked me to my office, where I located my own flashlight.

I called the on-call administrator. One of the hospital's administrators was always on call. I felt this was an unusual circumstance that administration needed to be aware of immediately. I reached the Director of Nursing. Pursuant to her direction, I contacted the power company for their expectation of when the power would be restored. I was informed that they had an employee "on the scene."

With my flashlight in hand, I started my rounds. I went first to ICU on the first floor. My primary concern was whether we had a patient on a ventilator. Fortunately, we did not. If there had been, nurses and the respiratory technician would have had to take turns "bagging" the patient, i.e. filling the lungs with air by squeezing an ambu bag attached to an endo tube. This action would have had to continue until the electricity was restored. With no patient on ventilator, I had little concern regarding that unit's patient care. We had three nurses working there who had the patients in their view, and could continuously assess them. ICU is shaped as a semi-circle with the nurses' desk centrally located. While each patient has an individual room, there are glass doors though which the nurse can see the patient, even if the door is shut. The nurses kept the doors open and, with flashlights, monitored the patients. I continued to the second floor to check the telemetry wing, where many of the patients were on heart monitors. Unlike ICU, each patient in the telemetry wing is in an individual room off a hallway. Data from heart monitors was displayed on a main monitor at the nurses' station (when the electricity was on). I emphasized to the telemetry nurses the importance of continually checking on the patients.

After about thirty minutes, Robin called to let me know that hospital maintenance had arrived. Good, I thought, this will be resolved soon. After speaking with Robin, I stopped in the ER on the first floor. The ER doctor informed me that he had called 911 dispatch and informed the dispatcher that Canonsburg Hospital was without power, therefore, we could not receive critical patients. This information would be relayed by dispatch to any ambulance services responding in the area.

I continued to the med-surg floors. As I walked through the dark halls, I could see the beams from flashlights, as the nurses checked their patients. With no electricity, the nurses would have no information from the heart monitors and patients could not activate a call light. I spoke with the nurses and assistants as I walked through the units. I told them to continually check their patients, especially the monitored ones. The staff was diligent in checking the patients, but naturally concerned about meeting patient needs in a timely manner. They asked me how long we could expect the power to be off. I informed them, "Maintenance is here and working the issue."

While I could not give the staff any estimated timeframe for the restoration of the power, I expected it would be within half an hour. That was not the case, however, and after a couple hours, the temperature had risen in the hospital. It was mid-summer and even at night, it was warm and humid. As I did continuous rounds, I could feel the beads of sweat on my body and observed that some patients had more difficulty breathing. There were flashlights located on each floor, and the staff were using these. However, after a couple hours, I was on my way to central supply, flashlight in hand, to get more batteries. The nurses pulled out the emergency supply of paper designed for nurses' notes. It had been many years since nurses wrote their notes hardcopy. Notes were now inputted into the computer and printed out when the patient was discharged. Without power, we had to go old school.

Around 2:30 a.m., I was informed that Robin was requesting me at the front desk. I again walked the dark stairs to the first floor, and as I approached the front desk, I could see a figure with a flashlight next to Robin. It was the maintenance man. Good, I thought. I was expecting him to give me the approximate time for the return of the electrical power and was hoping it would be soon. Instead he said, "The generators will not kick on. And the back-up generators won't either. I can't find the problem." I had no immediate response as my mind tried to process this information. As night supervisor, I felt I should have a plan not just for my staff to work in the conditions presented, but to take steps to remedy the condition. However, the condition was outside my realm. I tried to leverage the maintenance man's chain of command. I asked him to call his boss and advise him of the situation. Then I called the power company again. The person I spoke with informed me of the cause of the outage. She stated that a car had run off the road and hit a pole, damaging a transformer. With respect to estimated time of restoration, however, she could provide no information other than they were working on the issue. I then called the on-call administrator to inform her of the ongoing situation. She told me to call the hospital managers of each unit and inform them she was directing them to come in. There were four nursing units in the hospital, as well as ER, Pharmacy, and the kitchen. Each unit had an overall manager in charge of that unit 24/7. None of them worked nights, obviously. It was shortly after 3:00 a.m., and I began phoning.

When I got the groggy "Hello", I began: "Hi, this is Ruth from the hospital. We have a complete power outage, and the Director of Nursing has requested that all managers come in immediately. She wants everybody at their units." There was usually a pause here, as they processed the information. I had been working at Canonsburg for over thirty years at this point, and this was the first emergency all-manager report-in. After a moment, I would get a short dutiful confirmation. "All right; I'll be there." Within the hour, all managers were at their units. Their presence freed me to focus on the larger picture. I needed to ensure that the kitchen was able to address patient feeding, and I had to consult with surgeons who had surgeries scheduled that day. Meanwhile, the maintenance supervisor had obtained several smaller generators, and with the use of extension cords placed large fans in the hallways. The airflow was a relief to all.

I checked with the kitchen manager. This was not usually a unit I dealt with during night shift, but today was an exception. The electricity had now been off for four hours. The kitchen manager was able to plan a cold breakfast for the patients. She had also communicated with maintenance to request power of one of the small generators so she could make toast. With the kitchen situation in good hands, I went back to my office to deal with the issue of scheduled surgeries. Normally, the hospital had six to eight scheduled surgeries a day. The task of calling each scheduled surgeon and patient fell to me. I pulled the Operating Room (OR) schedule from my desk, and with my flashlight in my left hand, I began dialing with my right.

For each surgery, I contacted the surgeon first. I explained the power situation, and asked how they wanted to proceed. Some made the decision to cancel, while a couple wanted to keep the patient on stand-by with the hope that the electricity would be restored before the scheduled operation. I then called the patients and provided this information. All took it in stride. No one expressed frustration—that is until about 6 a.m. After I made my calls, I was going upstairs to make my last rounds. While the early morning sun was now beginning to lighten the sky, there are no windows in the stairwell. I saw the flashlight beam of someone descending. It was a surgeon from another hospital who also had patients at Canonsburg. When he saw me, he stopped and immediately began screaming at me. "If I can't do my surgery here soon, I will have to take my patient out to another hospital!" I told him that we hoped to have the situation fixed shortly, but I could not tell him when. It depended on the power company. He replied, "I'll see about this!" and stormed downstairs. While I completely understand his frustration, taking it out on me didn't make the solution move any quicker. Ultimately, he kept his patient at Canonsburg, and after the electricity was restored later that morning, the surgery was rescheduled for later in the day.

By the time I left that morning, the rooms were hot, the garbage had begun to smell, and the staff was beginning to be weary of the situation. Electricity was restored mid-morning.

I had worked through an earthquake, a building evacuation, and now a shift without electricity. To those entering the medical field, one word of advice I would give—always be prepared to work through the unexpected. Unlike most other career fields, we cannot pack up and go home when adverse conditions arise.

# CHAPTER 31

# *The Unexplained*

While I had experienced unexplained phenomenon with the changing on/off lights at the psychiatric facility in California, more unusual experiences awaited me in Canonsburg. In the older hospital, it mainly arose in an area on the third floor. This floor housed the ICU, a telemetry unit, and two med-surg wings—"Team 1" and "Team 2"—with a nurses' station in the middle. The issue belonged to Team 1's area. As the hospital supervisor, I was making my rounds on this unit, when the aides told me that they were afraid to go to the area in the end of the wing by themselves. I needed to know what had happened. The aides told me that the area was eerie and they had an unsettled feeling there. I didn't think much about this supernatural concern, and told them that when they needed to go to that area, they should do so together. Other concerns subsequently came from that same floor. Staff told me that equipment would be moved sometime during the night, yet the few staff members there swore they had not touched the item.

This activity apparently continued on the third floor after we had moved to the new hospital. Until the old hospital building could be sold, the administration decided to have a security guard on the premises. Thus, for several weeks, a security guard was the sole person at the old hospital building at any given time. When the new owners took over, the security guards assumed duties at the new hospital. I was at a nurses' station talking to some of the staff, when the night guard stop by and told us his story. He said he was glad to be at the new hospital; the old hospital spooked him out. One night while he was there alone, he was on the third floor sitting at the nurses' station when an elevator arrived on the floor. He wondered who was coming; he had not noticed anyone arriving at the hospital, and was not expecting anyone. He heard voices and laughter coming from the elevator, and assumed several persons were about to exit on the third floor, so went over to see who it was. He walked the short distance to the elevator and found it open but empty. We told him that we knew that floor was haunted. Being relatively new, he was out of the loop on that information, or I suspect he wouldn't have chosen that floor to work on.

While these few incidents happened on my shifts at the old hospital, I was surprised to find that even more unexplained activity would occur at the new hospital. Like my experiences at the psychiatric facility, many of the occurrences involved lights, this time call lights. There were times after a patient died and had been prepared for transport to the morgue, that his or her call light would turn on when no one was in the room. The call lights are visible above the patient's door and at the nurses' station. Early in my career, I learned an old superstition. After someone has died, a window should be opened to let the spirit out. I noticed that the older staff always did this, regardless of the weather outside. In the beginning I thought this was strange, but eventually I found myself adopting this ritual.

Once I was alone on a floor that was being renovated. When I made rounds, I had to walk the entire building to ensure things were in order. This meant even walking through the closed areas. I was approaching a storage room that was formerly a patient room. It still had a working call light. As I approached, the call light came on. I was trained to respond promptly to call lights, but this night I kept walking. In fact, I picked up the pace. That incident, however, was not the most unusual call light incident in the hospital. As I made rounds one night, a floor nurse told me her experience. She was at the nurses' station, when a call light came on. The system has an audio line to the room. So, she hit the button and said, "Can I help you?" A female voice answered, "My husband needs pain medication." She brought the medication to the room. There was no one but the non-communicative patient there. She wondered where the wife had gone. When she checked the patient's chart, she found out that the wife was deceased. I can't say that I was overly surprised; most of the unusual activity came from this same wing.

On different occasions, staff reported seeing an apparition going down this wing. Once, the observer was a new employee. I was in the nurses' station, when she approached me. She had a strange look on her face. She seemed to want to tell me something, but was reluctant to speak. I asked her if something was wrong. Then she told that she had seen a white form floating down the hallway. I'm not sure what reaction she expected from me. By that time, all I could say was, "Well, that's our resident ghost." It may sound odd, but I was disappointed it never appeared to me. After many years of night work, you would like to have one of these experiences that take you out of your routine, and further reaffirm your part of this unique work community.

As night supervisor, I received other reports of unusual activity. I was on the second floor when two nurses returned from break. From their faces I could see that something was wrong. Mentally, I was ready to instruct them in medical procedures or assist with a difficult patient matter. But their matter was beyond my professional knowledge. They explained that deciding to get some extra steps in on a break, they walked through an area closed for renovation. They informed me that the area was cold and had a strange eerie feeling that they could not explain. They said they would never go back there again.

They weren't the only staff to refuse to go to a certain area of the hospital. One hospital supervisor said she would not go back into the staff dining room. She explained that one night, when she entered alone, a heavy cart with a toaster on it started moving away from the wall and towards her. She screamed and ran out.

On one of my shifts, the guard and the housekeeper told me that they had both heard loud moaning noises coming from the main kitchen. They asked me if I had heard it. I had not—that is, until later that same night. I had to go through the kitchen to get to the supply room. When I was in the supply area, I heard the noise. I thought the guard and house-keeper were playing a joke on me. I quickly got my supplies, and I looked for them as I hurried out of the kitchen and into the hallway. No one was there; I neither heard nor saw anyone leaving. Many times prior to this, I had felt that I was being watched when I was alone in the kitchen. This incident did not help lessen that feeling.

Such occurrences went one step stranger when what seemed corporal appeared and disappeared. One of the nurses I supervised explained to me that she had some patient charting to do. To work undisturbed, she went to use the computers on a unit that was currently closed. There were no patients on the unit and no other staff. As she was doing the charting, she looked up and saw a man wearing a coat and hat. She thought he must be lost. As he approached, she asked him, "Can I help you?" He looked at her but did not reply. He turned around and started walking away. She watched as he vanished into thin air. She stopped charting, left that unit, and called me. At the end of her story, she looked at me earnestly, "I saw him! I'm not lying!" At that point in my career, I simply replied, "I believe you. I think you should finish your charting on your regular unit." There's not much other advice I could give. They did not teach this subject at South Side.

A similar incident occurred to a young guard. He had just left the dining hall in the North wing. The North wing at one time had been a skilled nursing unit, and still had its own dining room. It was now a rehab unit. He informed me of an elderly lady sitting in the dining hall. He explained that she was wearing a dress, not pajamas or attire a patient there would be wearing. He said he didn't know who she was but wanted to let someone know. So, I accompanied him into the dining hall. No one was there. We would have seen her had she left; the only other door out would have tripped the alarm. Nonetheless, I searched the area. Finding no sight of her, I asked the nurses if there was a visitor on their unit. They said no. I asked them if they had seen the woman. Again, they said no. So, I turned to the guard and gave him my best explanation. "It must have been a ghost." I could tell he was fairly new to the night shift by the spooked look on his face. More experienced night shift guards were not so shaken by such events.

One of these older guards was a minister of a small church, and he did guard duty for the extra money. One day another staff member was describing to us his observation of the white form, when the guard matter-of-factly one-upped him. The guard told us that on several occasions when he was in the hospital's morgue area, he saw shadowy human-shaped forms going in and out of the walls. I could not beat that one. My unexplained changing lights did not even come close.

# CHAPTER 32

# *With a Little Help from my Friends (The Snowstorm)*

It was later in my career that I earned a tagline when I was introduced to other network employees—all due to a snow storm. Early afternoon before my last shift for the week, I looked out my picture window and noticed that it had begun to snow. It was February in Pennsylvania and I did not give it much thought. However, within the hour the snow began falling thicker and started to pile up. I kept checking conditions, and soon was concerned about my commute to work—still several hours away. I had a two-wheel drive with low clearance. I decided to walk to end of my street to see if the residential roads had been plowed. As I walked outside, I immediately noticed that it was a heavy wet snow—a good snowman-making snow. The streets had not been plowed, and the snow kept coming.

I normally took a nap in the evening and left for work at 10:30 p.m. It was mid-afternoon, and I had to make a decision. Had I been a regular staff nurse, I would have called off. The roads were not safely drivable.

I found out later that even if I could have made it down the residential streets, the main street through Canonsburg, Pike Street, was closed due to the conditions. There was no reasonable way I could commute to work. Yet, I was a hospital supervisor; the overall operations of the hospital were to be under my watch that night. If I called off, no one else would be able to replace me, and the evening supervisor would have to pull a double. I also knew that of the supervisors, I lived the closest to the hospital—two miles.

I decided I would walk. I knew I would have to give myself extra walking time; conditions were worsening. I was now 69 years old; this would not be easy.

It was already dark outside before I left. I decided it was best to let someone know that I would be out in the storm . . . just in case. I called my son Allen, who lived a mile away from me. Not unexpectantly, he replied, "You can't walk there!" He explained how bad the conditions were outside, but I brushed off his concerns. I had already made my decision. A few minutes after I hung up the phone, it rang again. It was my daughter Beth. Allen had called for backup, and I was now receiving an admonition from her. Two against one, but I held my ground. I felt I was needed at the hospital. Beth said that if I was set on walking, at least I should have Allen accompany me. I told her I had never said he could not. So, a few minutes after hanging up from that call, I received a call from Allen. He started, "Are you *still* going to walk?" When I confirmed, he said he was going to walk with me, but asked that I meet him part way—at the gas station on Pike Street. I agreed.

I packed my uniform in a duffle bag. I threw in my lunch bag and set my purse out. I dressed in sweats and bundled up with a long coat, hat, scarf, gloves, boots. The snow was sticking to my coat before I was out of my driveway. The first mile was mostly downhill, but the second mile would be primarily uphill. I trudged down my street. Both the streets and sidewalks were covered with over a foot of snow. Knowing that some of the sidewalks had uplifted slabs, I chose the streets. There were no cars, no people, just the snow and me. It took me about 40 minutes to get to the gas station. I did not see Allen when I arrived. The snow was coming thick, and it was hard to see in the distance. After a couple of minutes, I saw a figure approach—Allen, of course. I was glad for his company. We had the uphill to go together. We exchanged a few pleasantries, but could not carry on a conversation in the snow storm. It was hard to see, and I kept my face downward to avoid the snow on the little skin I had exposed. My son and I walked side by side. We slogged up the long hill toward the bridge near the hospital.

About 90 minutes after I had left home, I walked in the hospital employee entrance, and brushed the wet snow off my coat. I had Allen follow me back to my office and got him a snack from the vending machine. He declined a warm drink but took a cold coke. He had another two miles to go, as he planned on returning home immediately. He told me that on his way back, it was somewhat odd being the only thing moving outside. On his arduous walk home, he heard loud crackling and looked to see sparks shooting from a transformer on the top of a telephone pole. Following this, a section of the neighborhood lost power. This occurrence repeated itself two more times on his walk home. The record setting storm had quickly dumped nearly two feet of heavy wet snow and caused wide-spread power outages. The media labeled it "Snowmageddon."

I took off my wet clothes and placed them around the office to dry. Dressed in my uniform, I then let the supervisor know I was there, so if she wanted to try to leave early, she could. Some employees, particularly those with 4-wheel drives, did venture home; others stayed overnight. The pharmacist stayed and slept in the pharmacy. I allowed the nurses and aides who stayed to sleep in empty patient rooms. With many of the staff calling off, some of the evening shift had to pull a double.

By the next morning, the main roads had been plowed, and most of the day shift staff were able to make it to the hospital, although some a bit delayed. I was relieved by the day shift supervisor and left the hospital at 8 a.m. I started my walk home. I did not call my son, as I knew it would have been dangerous for him to try to drive his car down the steeper unplowed residential streets. I started out. The snow was even deeper than when I came the day prior. My first fall was on the hospital grounds. But I kept walking. I had completed my last shift for the week and had two days off. I was walking home.

I fell a few more times, and wondered how I would make it up that long hill to my house. I had walked about a kilometer when my cell phone rang. It was Becky, my son Randy's fiancée at the time of his death. We were still close; I considered her part of the family. She said she called my house and I did not answer, so she was checking on me via my cell phone. I told her I was walking home and should be there in an hour. She directed me to stay where I was; her boyfriend, Pat—Randy's best friend during his life—had a new 4-wheel drive vehicle and would pick me up. I complied and got a most welcome ride home.

Not only did he drive me home, but Pat walked up to my porch, retrieved the snow shovel, and proceeded to shovel me a path to the door. His help did not end there, however. Most of Canonsburg was without power, and on my block, only a few houses had power. Luckily my house was one of these few. However, my son Allen's house was without power. When Pat found out later that morning, he went and picked up Allen, his wife and young son, and drove them to my house. I was half-asleep in bed when I heard Allen unlocking the door. They stayed with me for two days.

A few days later, I received a call from my boss. She told me I was going to be interviewed for the network newsletter. They wanted to ask me about my trek to work in the snowstorm, showing how I went above and beyond for work. I didn't think my walk was a big deal, truthfully, but was honored nonetheless. I was interviewed, my photo was taken, and the article appeared in the next newsletter. Thereafter, I was often introduced to other network employees as "that nurse who walked to work in the snowstorm." Looking back, I am grateful for the assistance I had both going to work and getting home. There is no replacement for having friends and family close by. I love my close community.

# CHAPTER 33

## *Rough Start to a Good Move*

"Is this hospital going to close?" It was 2013 and Canonsburg Hospital had just become part of a much larger network with a broader geographic footprint. As I did my rounds, I heard the same question over and over. I responded that we would remain a vital part of the network. Employees were still anxious about their jobs; there were rumors. In honesty, I had concerns also, but I kept these concerns to myself.

Shortly after we joined the larger network, corporate tried to assuage these concerns. Network officers held open meetings at the hospital. In these meetings they told us they planned to keep the hospital open, and tried to instill confidence in us by giving positive comments about the hospital. We were told, for example, that our hospital had good accessibility, as it was located near two major highways. While these meetings were positive, the staff remained concerned. They continued to hear otherwise from unofficial channels. With nearly 50 years of nursing, I wondered whether I would retire if the hospital closed. I had hoped to work a couple more years. Despite my many years of experience, I thought that given my age, I would be at a disadvantage in seeking another position.

Patient care went on as normal, and extra duties were given to nurse managers and supervisors. We were given handheld computers on which we had to input data on a daily basis. We were to visit a certain number of patients each shift every day, especially those patients in isolation and the elderly. There were several items we looked at, such as whether there were mats on the floor, whether the bedside table and call bell were within the patient's reach, whether the whiteboard was up to date. The data was collected, and our VP of Nursing received a report. We would discuss the data at our management meeting.

Changes were made to the delivery of the shift-change report. This had been done at the nurses' station or in the room behind it. Now, the report was to be given in the patients' rooms. For each patient assigned to a nurse, she and the oncoming nurse would enter the patient's room and discuss that patient while in the room. The supervisors had to observe a certain number of these reports and document data on a form that we turned in to our boss. I would check off items such as whether the nurse introduced the on-coming nurse to the patient, whether both nurses checked the IV site and dressings, whether the outgoing nurse stated when medications were last given. This was just more busy work for me. I trusted the nurses to give proper information at the shift change. Further, I had to try and get out of the office in time to catch these staff reports. This was sometimes difficult, as I had to get my supervisor's report first.

While I soon adjusted to the new procedures and the hospital did stay open, my fears turned in a different direction as the new hospital CEO started thinning the ranks of the current administration and bringing in others. I saw several of my colleagues retire or leave, one after the other. Soon it was just me and a couple of others from our pre-network days. I remember passing one of these individuals, a day-shifter, in the hallway one day. She looked at me, and said, "You're still here!" I replied, "Yeah, and so are you." Then we expressed our exasperation in a laugh.

The new CEO also managed to insult and ultimately disband the hospital's auxiliary. Canonsburg Hospital remained a non-profit hospital, and it had an auxiliary of volunteers. They ran a gift shop and a lunch counter during the day and evening. The lunch counter was popular; it was frequented by both visitors and locals stopping in for a meal. The lunch counter sold typical American fare—breakfast dishes, hamburgers, sandwiches, soups, shakes, homemade pies and other deserts. The auxiliary also selected rotating vendors that were permitted to set up in an area in the front hallway. These vendors sold various items, such as books, jewelry, purses, and children's gifts. The auxiliary received a percentage of the sales. All its profits were donated to the hospital for designated needs, such as beds, monitors, and other medical equipment. The auxiliary had been operating since the hospital opened.

The auxiliary's main fundraiser, a Christmas basket raffle, was held the last week of November and the first week of December. Each department donated a large gift or basket of gifts. The supervisors' office always donated one. Community businesses also donated items. The baskets were placed on tables, in a very festive display, in the front hall. An auxiliary member was present during the day. Staff and visitors would purchase tickets and put them in the container by the baskets they preferred. There was also a 50/50 drawing. This fundraiser had been held for several years. It was cheerful and brought some additional spirit to the hospital before the holidays. And from the donations given by the auxiliary, the hospital was able to buy needed equipment.

While I had always desired a day shift, there was now one major advantage to the night shift. I had little interaction with the new CEO. And when I did, I was prepared for her demeanor. I had heard many tales from the 3-to-11 supervisor and others; the first came the night after the new CEO started. At shift change, the 3-to-11 supervisor informed me that the auxiliary volunteers had complained of a very unpleasant encounter with the CEO. When the CEO saw the gift baskets, she screamed, "I will not have my hospital looking like a flea market!" She demanded that the auxiliary get rid of the baskets. One of the directors explained to the CEO that they could not get rid of the baskets. These were all donated, and people had taken chances on them. Others spoke to her about the fundraisers. She finally agreed the baskets could stay but there would be no more sales in her hospital. The auxiliary was compelled to cancel agreements with vendors.

This CEO then succeeded in closing the auxiliary's gift shop. The gift shop was manned by volunteers. Many were retired persons. There were also high school students who we referred to as "candy stripers" because of the red and white striped aprons they wore in the shop. One day the 3-to-11 supervisor told me of another incident, this one in the gift shop. The CEO put her rudeness on full display directly towards one of these young candy stripers. The CEO apparently did not like some aspect of her clothing, and went into a rant. The auxiliary had had enough of the CEO. They were volunteers and did not have to put up with her behavior. The volunteer-manned gift shop closed, and was replaced by a self-checkout machine. Morale was declining.

Tales of the CEO were being whispered throughout the hospital. Some people joked, with a heavy underside, that she must be off her meds. On one occasion, nurses who worked a twelve-hour shift, 7-to-7, informed me that the CEO had screamed at staff in a location where patients could hear her. As an RN taking care of patients, I found this beyond unprofessional. Once, as I did my rounds, the nurses on a med-surg floor informed me of a patient's apprehension after hearing such screaming. The patient had been admitted from the ER and told the nurse on the med-surg floor that she was concerned about staying at the hospital, because a woman working in the ER was screaming angrily at the nurses' station. The patient indicated that she almost declined admission. When the nurse checked with the staff, she found out it had been the CEO screaming. I felt an obligation to speak to the patient and reassure her. After I introduced myself, she repeated her story to me. She said she was afraid as to what would happen if she stayed at the hospital. I apologized and explained that she would be very safe. I further explained that the woman at issue would not be in the hospital at night.

Working nights, I was spared the frequent encounters the day shift sustained with the CEO. But I was not exempt. One night around midnight she called me from her home. She wanted me to investigate something that she said happened on 3-to-11. I was told to bring the report to her office that morning at 7 a.m. I do not know why she did not have the 3-to-11 supervisor investigate. The matter concerned a staff member allegedly napping in a bed in one of the closed units, between shifts. I asked staff members if anyone had knowledge. I prepared the report, and went to her office at the close of my shift. I expected a ten-minute meeting. It was forty-five minutes later when I left her office. I would never forget her pointing her finger at me and saying, "I don't care what happens to this hospital. I will always have a job at corporate. You and everyone else will have to find a new job." Given what I had witnessed and heard of her behavior, I honestly was not surprised at her uncaring attitude.

As a supervisor, I felt as if I were between a rock and a hard place. I should address unacceptable behavior in the hospital, but it was of the hospital's CEO. I felt I had no one to go to. This dilemma was compounded with the fact that she started replacing people in administrative positions with her previous colleagues. When I went to work each night, I never knew if it would be my last night there. After a year of her presence in the hospital, the majority of administrators had been replaced. I don't know what saved me—probably partly that I worked night shift, away from her immediate ire, and partly that I was one of the few with a master's degree, something I knew she desired in the administrators. In fact, she would not rely on personnel records as to our educational degrees and mandated that administrators bring in their actual diplomas. I had to go find not only my master's diploma, but my undergrad as well as my old South Side diploma.

I had planned to work a couple more years, and despite the difficulties the new CEO brought, I made the decision I would not leave. She would have to fire me. I had been through decades of nursing, through a lot of managements, and I was still around. I would not leave the job that I loved because someone else could not do hers.

While I was resolute in my decision to stay, the changes did have an effect on my health. With all the stress at the hospital, I was hospitalized with high blood pressure. They thought I was having a stroke but all my tests were negative. I was put on medication which controlled it.

After the new CEO had been there about a year and half, managing to get rid of most of the administration, extinguish the auxiliary, and frighten patients, she left with a short notice. On her last day, she arrived early for a 7 a.m. meeting. As she passed my office, she stopped and said, "Good morning." She was all smiles, and told me it was her last day. I wished her well. She gave me a hug as if we were friends and left. I was happily surprised. Hopefully her replacement would be professional. With the CEO's departure, there was a certain release of tension throughout the hospital. A couple weeks later, two other administrators and I were talking to a representative from the network who was filling in until a new officer could be assigned. She told me that she was sorry, no one was aware of the problems that had developed with the CEO. I was glad that I could now get back to fully focusing on my duties and the new policy changes of the network, without the troublesome disruption.

# CHAPTER 34

## *New Network*

Inclusion in the network brought many changes, including manage-ment techniques. A couple years after we joined the larger network, all supervisors and unit directors were required to attend a meeting regarding a network-wide concept that we would be implementing. I was curious as to what this concept would be. At the meeting, we were informed we were going to be having "huddles" with the staff on every shift. We were informed that this technique was being used at one of the large hotel chains with great success. Each week I would go into the network's website and print out the schedule for the week. It included a positive quote for the day, new information regarding the health sys-tem, and any new policies or procedures for our hospital. The huddles were to last no longer than ten minutes. I would hold the huddles at the nurses' station usually on my second rounds. That way, the staff would have already seen their patients. After I spoke, I would let the staff talk about any problems they wanted me to bring up at a manag-ers' meeting. I invited this, and I felt this was one of the most useful aspects of the huddle. The nurses seemed to feel comfortable speaking to me regarding any concerns. I was required to take attendance at the huddle, so I would have the staff sign an attendance sheet. This was the one aspect of the huddle I felt was not necessary. We are professionals, and the attendance documentation requirement had the implication that the network management did not trust us to comply. It took time to coordinate with the staff and perform the huddles, especially if it was a busy night, but I tried to make it a positive time. While I found the huddles useful, they only lasted about a year. There was no official policy change, but the schedule stopped appearing on the webpage.

Another change for supervisors was our title. We were no longer "supervisors" but Hospital Operational Administrators, or "HOAs." We all received a new work badge with the new title. We used to joke about having a new title, more work, but the same pay.

The supervisor duties were becoming more managerial, less hands-on nursing. I welcomed this change. We no longer had to help with endoscopies at night. A surgical nurse was on call to come in and help the ambulatory care nurse with the endos. I had always thought that the supervisors should not be doing this type of work, as it could tie us up for up to an hour. We had to be free to respond to codes and other hospital emergencies. Additionally, RNs were also being trained to insert IVs. One day, after a management meeting, I was speaking with the acting CEO. She asked me why I, a supervisor, was doing IVs and blood transfusions. I replied simply that I had always been required to do these procedures. We never had an IV team at night. She said, "Well that's going to change. All nurses need to know how to start IVs, and we are going to teach them." I thought this was a great idea. It was soon accomplished. Some of the nurses, however, were apprehensive. Starting an IV on a person is very different than starting one on a training mannequin. It takes practice. If the nurses had difficulties, they could and would call me. A new device was being used to locate veins, through shining light along the arm. I would use this technique to show the nurses the location of the veins, but I was old school in my own technique. I liked to feel for the vein. That always worked for me. Overall, these changes left me with more time to focus on management, including our new tasks. Prior to this, there were nights that I felt like two people—a supervisor and a staff nurse—going back and forth between the two.

Other positive changes involved internal communication at the hospital. With the new health system, all administrators were issued cell phones for hospital use only. We had one to share among supervisors. When anyone needed me, they could call directly. Prior to this, they would call the switchboard, and the switchboard would contact my pager with the number I needed to call. I would then go to a phone to call. Now with the cell phones, internal contacts were much easier. Further, one of the supervisors loaded all the staff personal phone numbers into the phone. Now, from anywhere in the hospital, I could call off-duty employees regarding staffing issues. I used to have to do this from my office. Changing to cell phones saved time and steps. Another positive technology change was that each unit received a certain number of pagers for the staff to carry. When a patient activated the call light, it would signal at the nurses' station. Prior to these pagers, it would be answered by the secretary (day and evening shifts) or one of the nurses (night shift), who would then overhead page the staff or, especially at night, go find the responsible nurse on the floor. With the pagers, the staff could be paged the information immediately. This made for faster response time for the patient and it cut down on the noise of the overhead paging.

Supervisors were given one additional duty we had not expected. Whenever a funeral home employee came to pick up a body from the morgue, the supervisor was to meet this person in the morgue and ensure they were picking up the right body. Unfortunately, there had been a mix up which triggered this policy change. Given that the identity was in two places on the body—one taped to the chest and one on the shroud—I wondered how this happened. Fortunately, it was not on my shift.

There was one new policy that was not well-accepted by the night shift nurses and aides—no food or drinks were allowed at the nurses' station. The night staff had only two fifteen-minute breaks, and were accustomed to eating or enjoying coffee, water, or other drinks at their desks. Being that we had a limited number of visitors at night, this was one rule I let them slide on, but only for the drinks, and I was firm that they had to remove the drinks before 5:00 a.m., as morning management may be on the floor. The nurses and aides were careful about complying.

Another change, but one that made no sense to me, involved pen colors. Our director bought different color fine tip sharpies. Each supervisor was to choose a color and stay with it. I selected aqua, a lovely lighter blue. Each time we signed or initialed a document, we had to use our own color. We all did it, but to me it reminded me of grade school. I never knew the reasoning behind this requirement, as it was clear by the signature who had signed. Did she think we were signing for each other?

My least favorite change was the change in shift hours. Supervisors began working twelve-hour shifts. The new supervisors wanted them. They said it gave them more time off and they could work a second job at another place. I was now scheduled two twelve-hour and two eight-hour shifts a week. This was hard for me. After working 11 p.m. to 7 a.m. for decades, my sleeping patterns were ingrained—a few hours in the morning and a few in the late evening. The change to twelves was physically difficult, but I had no option. Working a twelve-hour shift starting at 7:00 p.m. left me without half of my sleep. I never really got used to it, even after doing twelve-hour shifts for a couple of years.

There was one thing about the new schedule that I did like; however, it only lasted a few months. Because we had sufficient supervisors to cover shifts, I was asked if, once or twice a month, I would like to work one of my eight-hour shifts doing paperwork at hours of my own choice. I did not hesitate to accept. I was often coming in on my own time to complete paperwork. So, for this limited time period, once or twice a month, I worked one eight-hour shift, usually starting early afternoon, completing paperwork—cardiac arrest stats, updating the policy books, taking required training, and other work. I loved this opportunity to catch up on my paperwork uninterrupted.

The supervisors were no longer in charge of making their own schedule. The head of the emergency room made the schedule. Once she put me on four twelves in a row, and I told her that was too much for me. I was on my feet for most of the shift. When I raised the issue with her, I did have some apprehension. I wondered if my boss would encourage me to quit, if I could not pull four twelves. Fortunately, the head of the ER said she would see if she could rearrange the schedule, and she did.

There was one change which personally did not affect me, but was very difficult for some people—no smoking on the hospital *grounds*. The network sent out a mandate to all of their hospitals. Not only was smoking banned inside the hospitals but there was not to be any smoking on the grounds. This was not received well by the smokers. How would they get through their day? Our hospital had large grounds, and the policy applied throughout, including the parking lot and walking trail. Unlike the employees in the Pittsburgh hospitals, our employees could not simply walk a block away to smoke. On their breaks, some smokers would drive their cars off the property to have a cigarette. Some employees started having lunch at a fast food place, a couple miles away, so they could smoke in their cars. It was harder for night workers as they were not permitted to leave the grounds, and there was not a lunch period anyway. The staff had two fifteen-minute breaks. I knew that some of the staff parked at the farthest edge of the parking lot and would go there for a cigarette hoping not to be caught. Since I could smell the smoke on them when they returned, I would have to talk to them about it. Usually, they did not deny smoking, but complained about the policy. Some employees started using a nicotine patch. The policy applied equally to patients. It was tough for smokers, as we now had no place for them to go to smoke, not even outside. The staff would sometimes find patients smoking in the bathroom or standing by an open window blowing smoke outside. Then I would get a call to come talk with them. Unlike the smokers on the staff, the patients often tried to deny it. I would tell them, "If you are not going to listen, we are going to take your cigarettes from you." I felt like the high school teacher monitoring the halls, but someone had to do it.

# CHAPTER 35

## *The Rewards*

"Guess who was here today?" I was doing my first rounds and had just entered ICU. "I don't know. Who?" When they told me, I was joyfully surprised. I was so happy for him! When we had last seen him, the ICU nurses and I had assumed this patient would not survive. Several weeks prior, a man in his late thirties, had presented to the ER. He did not feel well, was weak, and had a fever. The doctor found that he had a serious infection throughout his body. He was admitted to a med-surg floor and was given intravenous antibiotics. Yet, his condition declined. He was then transferred to our ICU, where he stayed for a few days before being transferred to a larger hospital in Pittsburgh. While he was in our ICU, I would visit him at night and talk with him, but he was very weak. The nurses were sad when he was transferred, because we thought he was going to die. As with most transfers, we did not receive any news of his condition at the Pittsburgh hospital. We went on with our jobs. Now, several weeks later, the ICU nurses were excited to inform me that he had walked into our ICU earlier that day. He wanted to thank everyone for taking good care of him. He was completely recovered and, I was informed, smiling. It's those times that make you feel happy and proud to be a nurse.

The nursing profession brings with it a spectrum of emotions, including happiness and laughter, tears and sadness, and everything in between. One of the greatest moments is when someone you did not expect to recover stops by and says, "Thank you for helping me."

I found it particularly rewarding to see the progress of rehab patients. Improvement is often slow-paced, and it takes determination of the patients to continue working with the therapists day after day. I especially recall one patient, a woman in her forties, who was admitted to the rehab unit after suffering a massive stroke. Her left side was paralyzed and her speech was garbled to the extent it was not understandable. It was frustrating for her not being able to communicate and for the staff not being able to understand her needs. The rehab department worked with her several times a day. Each day, we saw improvement, incrementally. We all gave her encouragement. By the time she left, she was able to speak slowly and had gained some movement to her left side. I was amazed at how far she had come but knew she had a lot of rehab ahead of her. Yet, I knew that with her determination, she would further progress. The staff felt a sense of accomplishment knowing that they had helped her on the road to recovery.

On another occasion, I had received the shift report and was reviewing the patient census, when a name popped out to me. A friend of mine was on the list. She was both my neighbor and fellow church member. We often drove to church events together. She had a strong passion for life. She was one of those people with whom you never had to worry about a lull in the conversation. I enjoyed her friendship. When I saw her name on the list, I changed the order of my rounds, so I could get information on her earlier. While she was in her seventies, she was healthy for her age. She ate a healthy diet and exercised. She loved to take walks in the park. She had presented at the ER with generalized weakness; her legs were so weak she could not walk. She was awake when I entered her room. I talked to her, and told her I would check on her every night. Even if she were sleeping during the night shift hours, she could know that I had been there. The doctor had ordered a series of tests, and the results soon came back with unfortunate news. She had Guillain-Barré syndrome, a rare autoimmune disorder that damages the nervous system. After the diagnosis, she was transferred to ICU. By this time, she could not move her legs, and was showing signs of pneumonia. I would always encourage her and talk in a positive manner, but I really did not think she was going to live. She was transferred to a hospital in Pittsburgh for extensive therapy. Thereafter, she entered a rehab facility. I did not see her again for a few months. When she returned home, I visited her. She was weak but walking, and I was glad to find that she was back to her chatty self. She told me all about the long days of rehab, and how she found the pool therapy the most helpful. She said she was grateful for the care she had received at Canonsburg Hospital. She also said that her doctor in Pittsburgh told her that it was our accurate diagnosis and early start of treatment that helped her. That made me happy for her and proud of our hospital.

# CHAPTER 36

# *Retirement*

It was January 2017 and I knew it was time for me to retire. I had been a practicing nurse for more than half a century. I had seen major break-throughs in medical technology, the lifting of gender restrictions in the medical profession, and the expansion of specialties for nurses. The one change that I found dismaying, however, was the business focus overarching health care.

Health care had become big business with insurance companies at the head. They called the shots. They told hospitals whether a patient could be admitted and how long they could stay. While in the 1990s, the insurance companies did affect the length of a patient's stay through specific payment methods, the changes I saw in my last couple years of nursing were more intrusive in medical decisions. Normally, an ER doctor would contact the patient's attending physician for consultation on patient admission. In the last few years of my career, insurance applied network-specific, i.e. insurance did not cover treatment in all facilities. Thus, if a doctor felt that a patient needed to be admitted, the staff would have to determine which hospitals the insurance covered. Often the staff would then call another hospital that accepted that insurance to see if they had a bed available.

The changes also affected outpatient visits. Doctors were told how long they could spend with the patients in their office, since they were to see a certain number a day. My own family doctor retired, because he didn't want to follow these rules that limited his time with patients. He told me, "I will not have someone tell me how to run my office." My family was sorry to see him retire. He had seen my parents, me, my husband, and our children. Two of my adult children, still within the local area, continued to see him until his earlier-than-expected retirement.

As I typed my letter of resignation at home, I felt relief. I had found my career professionally satisfying, but was completely ready for a new chapter of my life. And at age 76, I was starting to feel exhausted by the twelve-hour shifts. I gave my retirement date of March 31, 2017, slightly less than three months away. I came to work carrying three copies of the letter—one for the Director of Nursing, one for Human Resources, and one to my boss, the Director of the ER. I left the letters at their offices, where they would find them in the morning. In the letter, I thanked them for their support. With each letter I dropped off, a positive feeling arose in me. I was looking forward to retirement.

At 5 a.m. on that same shift, I began my daily staffing calls. As night supervisor, I was responsible for ensuring adequate staffing—nurses and aides—for the 7 a.m. shift. The change to scheduled staffing depended on two factors—whether anyone had called off and the patient census. Thus, I was not always calling someone to come in unscheduled, but also informing staff that they were not needed for a shift. Both the aides and the nurses had a union, and we had rules for calling order. I could not call before 5 a.m., as this was considered too early. And I could not call after 5:30 a.m., as this would be rather late to inform someone whether they were needed for the 7 a.m. shift. Thus, I had a narrow window—one I could not always hit, as I had to respond to codes. As I made my calls that early morning, I could see the light at the end of the tunnel. I now had a specific number of times left that I had to do this task, one of my least favorites.

I had almost three months to clean my file drawers. In the supervisors' office, two long file drawers were mine. It may not sound like much, but one can cram a lot of documents into file drawers. I had kept a copy of everything I had to turn in. I learned early in my career to save a copy of all such documents. I had training and policy documents, evaluations of the IV team members, cardiac arrest data, minutes from meetings, reference books, and other miscellaneous material. When I could get a break on the night shift, I would try to make it through a file or two. Each file brought up memories of events and people. I found myself reading certain documents. In the minutes from the management meetings, I would see names of people no longer at the hospital. I paused as I thought of them. Overall, however, I didn't slow down my work just because I was retiring. But I did count down the days and check them off my calendar!

A few days before I retired, I received a memo for a mandatory meeting at 11 a.m. in the conference room. I thought, "Why do I have to go?" Anything new would not affect me. When I asked around, no one seemed to know what the meeting was about. So, I drove to the hospital, with no information on the meeting topic. When I walked into the room, everyone yelled, "Surprise!" It was a retirement luncheon for me. I couldn't believe that I hadn't got wind of it. My info gathering skills were slipping! It was a lovely lunch, and I was presented with many gifts. Then at noon, the doors opened and hospital staff started coming in to wish me well and enjoy cake with us. Even some off-duty employees came, as well as some of the doctors. It was a gratifying moment.

I had another surprise coming. Two nights before my retirement I was called to the west wing. They needed to see me. West wing was telemetry, and I was prepared to advise on whatever problem that had arisen. When I went up to the unit, however, I found a room full of staff, including several who were off-shift and had come in just for the farewell. They had brought farewell gifts and lots of food.

On my final night, I spent a lot of time talking to everyone. Fortunately, we had no codes that night. At the end of my shift, I gave my very last shift report. Then I clocked out for the last time and put my keys and badge on the desk. I no longer would carry the "keys to the kingdom." I headed down to ICU as they wanted to see me before I left. When I walked through the door to ICU, I was met with hugs and a large vase of yellow roses from Joyce. Then four of the ICU staff escorted me out of the building. As we said goodbye in front of the employee entrance, they threw confetti over me. I laughed. It was a nice touch to end the last shift of my career.

I knew I had made the right decision when I walked through the hospital a week later to post my thank you notes. During my career, whenever I came to work on an off-day for a meeting or to complete paperwork, I felt a certain responsibility. It was my hospital, and I wanted to know what was going on. When I walked in the week after I retired, however, that need was no longer with me. That part of my life—both rewarding and trying—was over. I will always be a nurse in my head and my heart, but it was time to start a new journey and see what adventures life would bring.

# POSTSCRIPT

A year after I had retired, I was reading the local paper when a photograph of the old hospital annex caught my eye. The article explained that the old nurses' residence had been renovated into apartments. An open house was announced. I felt compelled to go and see the place one more time. A couple days later, as I was walking into the old building, I ran into two old night shift colleagues on their way out. One of these nurses had graduated from the Canonsburg Hospital School of Nursing, and she said that she had to come to see what they did to her old room. I understood, as I was there out of a similar desire. I wanted to see my old office. The three of us stood outside the building and reminisced.

A new entrance with a porch had been added to the old annex. The glass-enclosed walkway had been removed. The main building remained a skilled nursing facility. The two buildings, now completely separate, served different purposes. I entered the designated entrance for the open house. A few people were looking around; I saw someone leading a tour on the first floor; and there was a room with refreshments. Feeling like I belonged there again, I walked past all of this and took the stairs to the second floor. I decided to give myself a tour. I walked down the hall and looked into the empty apartments. I was impressed. I particularly liked the size of the kitchens. It all looked so bright and new. Then I walked down to where my office used to be. The door was open. It was a laundry room. It was a disappointing moment to know that the office where I had spent many hours of my career was reduced to a laundry room. Ah well, time moves on.

After seeing the laundry room, I went down to the refreshment area. I introduced myself to the couple who were representing the apartment complex. I let them know I was curious about the place because I had worked in the building when it was the hospital annex. They had questions for me. They asked about the old layout, and how it used to be when it was the hospital annex 35 years prior. The man explained that he was involved in managing the skilled nursing facility next door, and asked me if I had seen it lately. When I said no, he asked if I wanted to see it. So, we walked over through the parking lot. No more enclosed walkway. He asked if I knew the Director of Nursing; she had worked at the Canonsburg Hospital. I did. He said, "I'll take you to her office; we'll surprise her."

When we arrived at her office, she was on the phone. She looked up and acknowledged me. When she hung up the phone, we hugged each other and talked for a while. Just before I left, she said, "Do you want a job?" Without hesitation, I replied, "No." While I loved my nursing career, it was now complete. There were other paths ahead of me I wanted to pursue.

While my career is complete, the instincts and compassion gained through the journey will never leave me. Part of me will always want to assist others in time of need. I will always be a nurse.

# ACKNOWLEDGEMENTS

*With special thanks to my daughter, Rhonda Bershok, who not only encouraged me to write my memoirs, but through many writing sessions with me—and assigning me homework!—transformed my notes into this book.*

*And with appreciation to all my children, for their encouragement on my journey and their understanding during the many years I retreated to the basement after dinner to study for classes.*

*And with gratitude to my wonderful staff. Our mutual respect for each other created a pleasant work environment and sparked a synergy that enabled the most effective care and enhanced my professional satisfaction.*